SELF-EFFICACY:

RAISING THE BAR FOR ALL STUDENTS

Second Edition

Joanne Eisenberger
Marcia Conti-D'Antonio
Robert Bertrando

EYE ON EDUCATION
6 DEPOT WAY WEST, SUITE 106
LARCHMONT, NY 10538
(914) 833–0551
(914) 833–0761 fax

Library of Congress Cataloging-in-Publication Data

Eisenberger, Joann, 1942-
   Self-efficacy : raising the bar for all students / Joann Eisenberger, Marcia Conti-D'Antonio, Robert Bertrando.— 2nd ed.
         p. cm.
      Includes bibliographical references.
      ISBN 1-930556-95-0
   1. Learning disabled children—Education—United States. 2. Inclusive education—United States.
3. Learning strategies—United States. I.
   Conti-D'Antonio, Marcia, 1953- II. Bertrando, Robert, 1941- III. Title.

LC4705.C67 2005
371.9—dc22

                                                                              2004028877

Cover design by Carolyn H. Edlund
Editorial and production services provided by
Richard H. Adin Freelance Editorial Services
52 Oakwood Blvd., Poughkeepsie, NY 12603-4112
(914-471-3566)

Also Available from EYE ON EDUCATION

Helping Students Graduate:
A Strategic Approach to Dropout Prevention
Jay Smink and Franklin Schargel

Dropout Prevention Tools
Franklin Schargel

At-Risk Students:
Reaching and Teaching Them, Second Edition
Richard Sagor and Jonas Cox

Strategies to Help Solve Our School Dropout Problem
Franklin Schargel and Jay Smink

Applying Standards-Based Constructivism:
A Two-Step Guide for Motivating Elementary School Students
Flynn, Mesibov, Vermette, and Smith

Applying Standards-Based Constructivism:
A Two-Step Guide for Motivating Middle and High School Students
Flynn, Mesibov, Vermette, and Smith

Constructivist Strategies:
Meeting Standards and Engaging Adolescent Minds
Foote, Vermette, and Battaglia

Achievement Now!
How to Assure No Child Is Left Behind
Dr. Donald Fielder

Writing in the Content Areas, Second Edition
Amy Benjamin

What Every Teacher Needs to Know about Assessment
Leslie Walker Wilson

ABOUT THE AUTHORS

Joanne Eisenberger, has been in public education for 36 years. After two years in the Peace Corps in Liberia, she taught mainstreamed Special Education classes in Washington, California, New York, and Pennsylvania, and was 504 Coordinator in the Unionville-Chadds Ford School. A coauthor of *Supporting Students with Learning Needs in the Block,* she earned her Masters Degree in Special Education from San Francisco University.

Marcia Cont-D'Antonio is Director of Special Education for the Westchester Area School District. A coauthor of *Supporting Students with Learning Needs in the Block,* she has been in public education for 26 years with teaching experiences in elementary education and in special education K-12, as well as with the diagnosis of learning disabled students. She directed two federally funded projects to train educators to teach Special Education students included in their classrooms. She earned her Masters Degree in Special Education from Temple University and completed her graduate work in reading at University of Pennsylvania.

Robert Bertrando, a coauthor of *Supporting Students with Learning Needs in the Block,* was the Director of Secondary Education for the Unionville Chadds-Ford School District. He has been in the field of public education for 41 years, having begun his teaching career as an English/social studies teacher. He has been involved in designing and coordinating district initiatives to adapt curriculum and instruction to meet the needs of the diversified learner. He earned his B.A. from Pennsylvania State University and his masters degree from West Chester University.

Foreword

Instruction and student/teacher relationships are identified as significant dynamics impacting achievement in school. The importance of focusing and strengthening these critical interactions has received considerable attention from researchers in recent years. The complexity of strengthening instruction and student/teacher relationships is further challenged and complicated by the increased student diversity experienced in schools across the country. Successfully teaching diverse populations of students places additional demands on teachers struggling to prepare all students to reach the higher academic standards, knowledge, and skills required of 21st century citizens i.e., to sort competing ideologies, to utilize complex technologies, and contribute to a global economy.

Traditional practices of tracking, varied curricula, and reducing the diversity of the student populations in classrooms by segregating remedial, special education, and English language learners, will no longer meet the requirements of current reform policies and proposals demanding success for *all* students. A recent survey of teachers reveals however, that only 32% of teachers feel prepared to teach culturally and socioeconomically diverse populations of students or those who are learning disabled. In addition, despite the numerous school reform efforts of the 1990s, significant gaps exist in the academic performance of groups of students.

The *No Child Left Behind Act (NCLB)*, signed into law January 2002 by President George W. Bush, represents the major effort of the United States government to remedy these educational realities. The No Child Left Behind law relies heavily on standardized testing for students and accountability for schools and teachers. One major requirement of these policies and reform proposals is specific assistance to teachers who require deeper understanding and varied instructional strategies to engage diverse populations of students.

Responding to this challenge, the authors of this book offer a philosophy of *efficacy* that defines high teacher and student expectations. The instructional strategies delineated contribute to a *no excuses* model of student/teacher interaction that creates caring environments for learning. The definitions, examples, and strategies outlined will strengthen the abilities of parents, caregivers, and teachers to put energy into learning; to provide experiences that successfully motivate students who may be diverse because of poverty, cultural dfferences, or learning disorders. Implemented in concert with current reform strategies e.g., reduced class size, standards, research based programs, etc., teachers armed with knowledge and skills described in this book will make a major contribution to the effectiveness of an educational system that enables increased numbers of all groups of students, not just a few, to reach their potential.

Belinda Williams, Psy. D.
University of Pennsylvania

FOREWORD
IN PREVIOUS EDITION

We ask a lot from teachers. In truth, it cannot be any other way. Teachers are architects of lives. A human work-in-progress comes to school. Willingly or not, that child will spend the bulk of his or her prime waking hours in a classroom, working at the direction of a teacher.

The way in which that child experiences the classroom will contribute in important ways to whether the child hungers after learning or seeks to escape it, feels empowered or dehumanized, becomes part of a community of peers or is set apart from the group. There is great power in the role of a teacher and no teacher can avoid exercising it. What we *can* do as teachers is continually prepare ourselves for the wise use of the power that is unavoidably ours.

Teaching has never been easy. There have always been too many learners assigned to too few teachers. Learning spaces have always been too restrictive, materials too few. We have always been starved for time.

In addition, teachers encounter each day the most diverse student populations we have known. Students come from varied cultures which equip them with a wide array of lenses through which they view the classroom and life. Gender still shapes and separates us, with gender role variance compounding cultural and language variance. Some students come to us years ahead of the prescribed curriculum, while others are years behind it. Even advanced students may not excel in all areas, may do battle with emotional or behavioral demons, or may struggle with learning disabilities. And still, there are too many students, too few teachers, too little space and a dearth of time.

Excellence is a highly personal thing. To ensure each learner's access to personal excellence, we must come to understand how to meet each learner as he or she comes to us, and help that learner grow as far and as fast as possible. We need to help each learner extend and discover interests and talents. We must create environments that help each learner learn more about how to learn best.

Most of us will also need to develop a far richer reserve of strategies to help students develop the attitudes and skills of successful learning. We need not a hefty bag of tricks, but knowledge of what makes people successful. We must develop increased sensitivity to the great variety of impediments to personal and academic success. We need to figure out what stands between any student and the next increment of growth. We must also develop the skill to flexibly apply concrete strategies that help each learner exercise increased personal control of success.

We will also have to become much more comfortable with orchestrating multi-task classrooms with a consistent and purposeful mix of whole class, small group, and individual work; where time is flexible; and where learners share responsibility with the teacher for smooth functioning of the classroom. Since so many of us have become skilled at teacher-led, whole group instruction, this challenge is a significant one.

The authors of this book offer pedagogy for academically diverse classrooms. They provide concrete models for supporting student success and help us understand the intent of the models so that we can develop some approaches of our own.

This book is important to me because it builds scaffolds, not excuses, for teachers and students alike. It challenges teachers to do what students must also do—maintain the belief that we can achieve complex goals, persist in working toward those goals, and be resilient when the day does not go well.

The book evokes images of classrooms in which teachers and students are fiercely determined to maximize the possibilities of every person in the room, where teachers and students are increasingly savvy about how to make that happen, and where both are willing to work long and hard when success seems most distant. That's what all our classrooms ought to be like. This book helps us move in that direction.

Carol Ann Tomlinson, Ed.D.
The University of Virginia

PREFACE

Significant new changes have occurred in education. The legal mandates of No Child Left Bedhind (NCLB), the Individuals with Disabilities Education Improvement Act (IDEA '04), and Section 504 of the Americans with Disabilities Act (ADA) have become the legal mandates that now force educators to examine and improve the way access is provided to a Free and Appropriate Education (FAPE) to all students. We wrote this book to assist the educational community in making appropriate responses to the requirements of these mandates. The changes have also forced educators to examine their practice and test the limits of how inclusion of special-needs students impacts teachers, administrators, and other students on a daily basis. Neither NCLB nor IDEA '04 will go away. Elements may be modified through the courts, but they will not disappear. Waiting, as educators sometimes do, "for this to pass," will not serve the professional community well. When elements of the laws are tested in the courts, school districts must respond.

Although both NCLB and IDEA '04 have flaws, and opposition to elements of these laws can be heard in school board chambers, teachers' lunchrooms, and taxpayer group meetings, there is one fact that can not be debated. Special education has become everyone's concern, and the line between special education and general education has been blurred.

The general educator is affected most acutely because students with all types of learning needs are a part of the general curriculum and will be included in almost every classroom. Except for the most profoundly handicapped, all students now participate in State Stanstrds testing and are represented in NCLB reporting. The burden now falls on school districts to prove why a student should *not* be fully included.

This book focuses on what is necessary for all students to be successful. To achieve success, individuals must believe that they have the abilities needed to produce quality work through sustained effort. This definition of success is referred throughout this book as self-efficacy. This book gives us an opportunity to take the good and positive elements that have been learned from the practitioners in the field of special education to enhance learning for all students. When school districts embrace initiatives that improve learning by adopting high standards and rigor for all students, combined with opportunities for self-efficacy, then meeting the mandates of NCLB will not be seen as a separate process but as part of the natural context for quality general education.

Educators currently in the field as well as those in preservice will benefit from this book. We refer to specific instructional strategies for self-efficacy throughout the book, as well as to authentic student artifacts that we used when teaching for efficacy. We believe it is critical to communicate clearly to parents about progress in the general curriculum as well as what supports efficacious behavior in children. We include valuable information for working together with parents toward this goal of independence. The appendix has ready-to-copy black-line masters of the forms and Curriculum-Based Assessments that we use in our classrooms. Using these will let you go right to work.

TABLE OF CONTENTS

1

SELF-EFFICACY VERSUS SELF-ESTEEM

The regulations of No Child Left Behind (NCLB) and regualtions of the recently reauthorized Individuals with Disabilities Education Improvement Act (IDEA '04) continue to drive the nature and practice of education in the United States. States must include students with learning needs in their statewide and district wide testing programs and include their scores in school reports. The vast majority of students with all types of learning needs, including those in need of Special Education, must remain the shared responsibility of the general education and Special Education teachers. IDEA '04 is premised on basic beliefs:

♦ The majority of students with disabilities are best educated with their nondisabled peers.

♦ Students with disabilities must have access to the general curriculum, including the same skills, concepts, contents and understandings as their nondisabled counterparts.

♦ Students in both NCLB and IDEA '04 are required to progress. NCLB requires that schools make *adequate yearly progress*, IDEA '04 requires that students make *meaningful progress*.

The intent of both laws is clear. Schools must employ best practices to ensure that all students progress. Schools that have not demonstrated Adequate Yearly Progress (AYP) must now improve and children not making meaningful progress must do so. All teachers must expect high standards of performance from all students. General education teachers, who may be content experts, must now expand their educational knowledge, improve their lesson designs, and expand their instructional practices and assessment methods to allow the disabled not only to access the curricula they are delivering but to facilitate progress. Progress, once limited to summative evaluations and measured in factual objective tests, must be expanded to include ongoing progress monitoring, and teachers must remain vigilant to ensure that meaningful progress is made within the general curriculum as well as toward Individual Education Plan (IEP) goals.

NCLB and IDEA '04 have also redefined the curriculum, expanding the traditional definition to include multiple opportunities for students to show what they know, understand, and can do. General education is now defined as a continuum of outcomes and skills for all students ages 3 to 21. It involves all ofthe acivities, materials, instructional techniques, and objectives experienced by all students. While specific content knowledge is an integral part of all curricula, the requirements of inclusion have expanded the definition to include skills and processes as well as activities, materials, and instructional techniques. Teachers must now attend equally to content and process and be able to articulate both. Teachers join parents as central members within the education program (IEP) teams, using their knowledge of the curricular demands and requisites of the child, to develop learning goals for all education students. Parents and caregivers provide the cultural/experiential lens through which to view their unique child.

Because of IDEA '04 and NCLB, students with all types of learning needs may arrive in general education teachers' classrooms with deficiencies in the strategies that are important for academic, behavioral, linguistic and social functioning. Students with learning needs may not know how to approach tasks with an effective plan of action nor be able to estimate accurately how much time a task will require. They may not have the skill attitudes and dispostions necessary to be successful. Some of these students may exhibit disorganized thinking and have problems in planning, organizing and controlling their lives in academic and social settings. They may lack resilience and self-efficacy. Their school performance, when compared with their ability or their nondisabled peer group may be poor. This poor performance may be evidenced on report cards rife with D's and F's, by poor attendance or by discipline issues. The work that they do may be incomplete or of poor quality, which they may explain on personal terms. They may request adult intervention/help before making an attempt to improve their work, or they may avoid tasks completely by treating teachers and other adults as enemies to fight. They often have no strategies for comprehending, retrieving, or using information. They may attend high poverty schools. They may have a tendency to complete only work that is effortless and openly complain if work requires effort. They behave as though they have no autonomy over how they live their lives. These are students who have not developed self efficacy, the belief that they have the capabilities needed to produce quality work through sustained effort (Fig. 1.1). Because these students approach difficult tasks without self efficacy, they question their capabilities and make very poor use of their skills. However, with strategy instruction, students can make better use of their abilities. The student response in Figure 1.1 illustrates the power of strategy instruction.

Many general education students also evidence learning or behavior problems that call for specialized or remedial instruction in order to develop a sense of efficacy. Because these students have not developed a belief in the learning efficacy needed to activate and sustain the effort and thought required for skill development, many of these students are at risk for school failure. These students can be informally categorized according to the causes of learning interference, but they do not require Special Education and are still required to make progress under NCLB. These categories include children whose native language is not English, students who exhibit cultural differences, slow learning rate, and underachievement, as well as students with diagnosed learning weaknesses or health disorders such as attention deficit hyperactivity, and students who exhibit cumulative deficits or educational deprivation. Varied experiential backgrounds and/or inappropriate teaching, accompanied by some learning differences and weaknesses, account for the academic difficulties of these students. Without appropriate attention, these students eventually may become classified as disabled and enter burgeoning special education programs.

As members of the IEP team, special education and general education teachers will need to help parents recognize that the goal of IDEA '04 is to graduate productive, resilient, independent citizens to the greatest extent possible. Educators need to include parents in problem solving and goal setting so that efficacy training and reinforcement can occur at home as well as at school. Parents can provide the cultural/experiential lens through which their children can be viewed more completely by the school team. Teachers need to articulate the benefits of efficacious behaviors, provide concrete and accurate information about their student's progress, and be prepared to encounter opposition from parents and administrators as students who are accustomed to an *easy ride* express their complaints. Parents must also be supported as they struggle with the realization that appropriate but rigorous and demanding tasks need to be part of their child's education. For more information on working with parents see chapter five.

FIGURE 1.1. A STUDENT'S RESPONSE TO THE SAME QUESTION BEFORE AND AFTER STRATEGY INSTRUCTION

Directions: Explain how your learning styles and intelligence strengths affect your learning.

Before Strategy Training

> I think I learn better with groups because then I'm not depended on to do the whole project by myself. If I have a project I can fall back on my friends if I don't understand or need help, they would have the same topic.

After Strategy Training

> I am a visual learner. I believe that by highlighting, keeping assignments & tracking my graids I will remember the things & that by positive self talk, having a studdie partner, and requesting for help on tests I will become a better learner.

NCLB and IDEA '04 require teachers to be highly qualified. Special Education teachers will need to demonstrate competence in the content areas of instruction in which they teach to demonstrate that they have the content knowledge necessary to maximize their student's growth .If special education teachers are teaching students above the 6th grade learning level, they must demonstrate that they have the necessary content knowledge. Special education teachers must also expand their instructional and assessment practices so they can provide consultative support to fellow educators about how all students can be successful in general education classes. The learning support teacher must move away from a focus on tutorial to a focus on teaching for independence and mastery. Because their students will be educated in general education classes, learning support teachers must develop cooperative planning and cooperative teaching skills to support the general education teacher as they struggle to be successful with students with learning needs.

Many programs for students with learning needs have unwittingly contributed to the low efficacy of these students by responding too quickly with help that rescues instead of teaches and with excuses that remove accountability.

These practices are justified in the name of self-esteem when the effect of this behavior is to reinforce the students' sense of incompetence and dependence. The educators in these programs sometimes judge their success or failure with students by how happy and cooperative the student is. They may attribute their lack of success with a particular student to unfair or unrealistic demands of NCLB. With the best of intentions, some teachers, psychologists, and guidance counselors protect and enable students, allowing the student to avoid using the persistence and effort needed to do well in school and life. Unfortunately, it is not uncommon to see teachers spending most of their instructional time helping students complete homework and cram for tests instead of instructing students in the strategies that will be needed for social competence, self efficacy, independence, and academic progress. These teachers openly justify their behavior by explaining how the student feels, unwittingly reinforcing feelings of temporary happiness, long-term inadequacy, and an unacceptably high level of student dependency.

Meeting the demands of NCLB and IDEA '04 require a continuum of services for students with special needs. Some students must be taught how to face gaps in their knowledge, skills and competencies and be given experience with gaining control guided in managing school. Support teachers may still need to teach some students in small groups outside the content classroom in order to meet their unique needs. However, the focus of these groups can no longer be content area tutoring. If students are to succeed in school and enter society as independent adults, all teachers must see their role as teaching strategies necessary for independence. The benefits of such teaching strategies can be seen in the student response below (Fig. 1.2). For more exercises that promote self efficacy see chapter 3.

FIGURE 1.2. A STUDENT IDENTIFIES NEEDED STRATEGIES[1]

Directions: Pick two strategies to learn and tell why you need them.

Strategy #1 <u>chairs in place</u>

I will use this for: <u>chairs in place sounds like a good idea for taking tests. I realize that I need to sit alone when taking a test.</u>

Strategy #2 <u>pocket process</u>

I will use this for: <u>I have problems paying attention so that's why I picked pocket process so I can get back on track. I can't sit and not wonder off in la la land.</u>

Some general education teachers are unwitting partners in reinforcing poor performance by failing to hold students accountable or by using pedagogy that

---

1 For explanations of Chairs In Place and Pocket Process, see Appendix I: Strategies.

allows them to assume what should be students' responsibilities. General education teachers often avoid confronting the students, especially students with aggressive parents, and accept passive participation. The general education teachers, like the special education teachers, ignore behaviors that encourage low effort. Many of these behaviors were identified by Landfried (1989), i.e.:

- allowing students to tune out while the teacher does the talking and the thinking,
- consistently accepting forgotten assignments late or incomplete,
- giving credit for sloppy or partially finished work,
- ignoring cheating,
- allowing students who have not completed the basic work to pass courses with extra credit,
- giving easy tests, and grades that require little or no serious effort or study,
- accepting excuses from students (I had to work late last night), which avoid accountability,
- accepting excuses for poor performance from students with learning needs that would not be acceptable for the rest of the school population, and
- consistently accepting and explaining away discourtesy from students because of learning needs.

Some of this confusion and enabling behavior comes from a mistaken understanding of the role of self-esteem versus that of self-efficacy. Robert Sternberg (1988) makes the distinction clear. Every child becomes more self-efficacious when they accomplish something they didn't think they could. If you want mediocrity embrace self-esteem; if you want growth embrace self-efficacy. In fact, students may judge themselves inefficacious in a task without suffering any loss of self-esteem because they do not invest their self-worth in the activity (Bandura 1997). People may also be very efficacious but take no pride in their performance. Students who place a high value on social activities are not devastated by report cards that have Ds and Cs if they have consciously chosen to spend more time on social activities then on school activities. Neither a student's self-esteem nor his self-efficacy is boosted by an easy A.

Performance attainment, a necessary skill for school success, is the product of self-disciplined effort. Well-meaning teachers confuse the lack of performance attainment with self-esteem . When this confusion arises, students' poor performance is attributed to a lack of self-esteem when, in many cases, students actually lack self-efficacy. These students have an inaccurate judgment of their personal capabilities, an inability to regulate and monitor their application of skills and knowledge, and inadequate goal achievement.

FIGURE 1.3. THE CHARACTERISTICS OF SELF-ESTEEM AND SELF-EFFICACY ARE COMPARED

Self-Esteem	*Self-Efficacy*
Judgment of self-worth	Judgment of personal capabilities
Regulates happiness	Regulates acquisition of knowledge and skills
Self-liking	Self-discipline
Personal accomplishments	Performance attainment
Predicts satisfaction	Predicts effort and motivation
Product of social evaluation	Product of reflection
Produces contentment	Produces goal achievement

All teachers must build resilient efficacy in their students. Students who are participating fully in general academic programs, and for whom full participation in society is planned, must be able to apply what they know consistently and persistently, especially when academic, social or emotional progress is not going well. Building this efficacy requires that students experience overcoming obstacles through effort. Difficulties and setbacks actually serve a beneficial purpose. The struggle to overcome the obstacles teaches students that success usually requires sustained effort. If students with learning needs continually experience easy success, they come to expect quick results and are easily discouraged by failure. They give up quickly when faced with the smallest challenge. For academic success, teaching resilient efficacy is more important than modeling of strategies, cognitive coaching, or tutorial instruction.

Instruction in strategies and practice in applying the strategies will not improve academic achievement. But reminding and reinforcing students for exercising better control over academic, social and behavioral tasks by using the strategies will improve performance (Bandura, 1997). In other words, the more the special education and general education teachers can enhance the student's belief in his or her ability to exercise control over progress, the better the performance. Therefore, the most important role for the special education and the general education teacher is to provide the student with the rules and strategies needed to exercise control and to reinforce their students in applying the strategies for achieving their learning goals consistently and persistently.

Support programs and classroom remediation for students who fall behind must be designed to accelerate learning so students can make up deficits or learn the bypass strategies needed to rejoin the regular instructional and social life of the school. The student's progress should be closely monitored with quick corrective feedback given. The focus of the remediation and the teaching of replacement strategies or support should be to encourage the student to manage his or her own learning and to become self directed. For more information on the skills and strategies needed for academic, social and emotional success see chapter 4.

Experiencing success is an integral part of the process of building a strong sense of efficacy. Success builds personal efficacy and failure undermines it. This is especially true if failure occurs before a sense of efficacy is firmly established (Bandura, 1997). Special education teachers must, therefore, work closely with general education teachers during cooperative planning and cooperative teaching times. Working with content teachers to differentiate content, activities, and products in the content classroom to maximize the student's opportunity for success must become part of the learning support teacher's job. Support teachers must share their knowledge of students' strengths, diversity, and interests with the general education teachers so that differentiated assignments, based on interest, readiness, or learning profile can allow all students to maximize success while reinforcing a strong sense of self-efficacy. Exercises that allow students to make use of acquired skills, demand high level, quality thinking and persistence must be developed (Costa, 1985).

Even when teachers have attended to the diverse needs of the class by constructing lessons, tests, and other curriculum based assessments with extreme care, students with serious learning needs will require additional accommodations or modifications to demonstrate mastery of knowledge and skills. But the accommodations must be carefully constructed and appropriate to avoid undermining a developing sense of efficacy. It is important to note that IEP teams should make accommodations only when clear, objective evidence of need has been gathered from a variety of sources and across multiple settings. Some of these sources should include a variety of classroom observations, as well as standard, teacher made, and curriculum based assessments. The list of student's accommodations below is an example of one based on need (Fig. 1.4).

**FIGURE 1.4. A STUDENT'S ACCOMMODATIONS
ARE IDENTIFIED BY LEARNING NEEDS[2]**

Name _Paul Jones_   Date _9/12/99_ Disability _Auditory Processing/ADHD_

My Academic Strengths	*Successful Strategies*
Short-term Visual Memory	3-Fold Page, 2-Column Notes
Verbal Reasoning	Study Partner, Stop and Think
Visual Processing Speech (in gifted range)	Muscle Reading, Graphic Organizers

My Learning Needs	*Successful Accommodations*
Auditory Processing	Visual Format for Information, Directions
Impulsive	Firm Limits and Boundaries—Avoid Verbal Debates
Task Completion	School-Home Communication
Attention and Concentration	Proximity, Goal Setting, and Reflection on Progress

For copies of the strategies mentioned in the Accommodations see Appendix-Strategies. A reproducible copy of the Accommodation form is located in Appendix-Forms.

It is also critical to understand that the need for any particular accommodation can change over time. As a student matures, learns new skills, or when task demands change, a particular accommodation may no longer be appropriate. As the student learns and uses strategies that bypass weaknesses, a particular accommodation may need to be adjusted. An accommodation may be necessary and appropriate in one discipline but not in another. Because of the shifting nature of the accommodations, it is critical that special education teachers, general education teachers, and parents talk regularly and plan together.

If schools are going to meet the demands of NCLB, accommodations and modifications should never be used as a replacement for the time and energy students need to put into learning. Cooperating teachers who administer accommodations must be careful to avoid helping students to the point of cheating. Providing accommodations and modifications that reduce a student's op-

---

2 For copies of the strategies mentioned in the Accommodations, see Appendix I: Strategies. A reproducible copy of the Accommodations form is located in Appendix II: Forms.

portunities to build the skills needed for successful actions teaches dependence and passivity while reinforcing low efficacy. Accommodations and modifications are only appropriate if they do not invalidate the skill being taught or measured and if they do not jeopardize self-efficacy. Applying accommodations or modification inappropriately can actually cause intellectual self-doubt and prevent students from putting enough effort into their work. They can severely undermine a student's accurate appraisal of the time, effort, and resources needed for academic success (Bandura, 1997). Appropriately designed accommodations and modifications can increase self-efficacy by allowing a student to act on a sound appraisal of his or her personal capabilities and increase the prospect of success.

All professionals strike a balance between keeping expectations for performance high, but reasonable, without providing so much assistance that the student is crippled by enabling adult behavior (Conti-D'Antonio, 1998). The overriding message, especially for students who require accommodations and modifications, should be independence. For more information on accommodations and modifications see chapter 4.

Developing student efficacy is, in large part, dependent on the teachers' belief that they can be successful with difficult students or students in difficult situations. This belief translates into the way teachers construct their lessons, their methods of delivering instructions, and how they maintain order and control. Efficacious teachers know how to prevent disruption from occurring by establishing the classroom as learning communities where all styles, cultural backgrounds, and intelligences are honored. They maintain clear expectations, provide consistent structure, patience, and sustain routine rules. They listen to their students. These educators praise students for growth even when the growth is in small increments and they deal with inappropriate behavior quickly and firmly. Figure 1.5 compares descriptors of lessons prepared by teachers with high and low instructional efficacy.

FIGURE 1.5. COMPARING INSTRUCTIONAL EFFICACY

Teachers with High Instructional Efficacy	*Teacher with Low Instructional Efficacy*
Believe all students are teachable	Give up quickly on students
Expect learning to require sustained effort	Create engaging but not effective, fun tasks
Teach appropriate strategies	Focus on dispensation of facts
Provide feedback and praise	Criticize and point out failures
Use persuasion, rigor, and intrinsic interests	Use coercive, punitive, and negative sanctions
Focus on student development	Focus on subject matter
Emphasize mastery experiences	Emphasize control and regulation

---

The more instructional support and technical assistance teachers receive in managing their educational activities, the better their sense of instructional efficacy. Schools that support and enhance teachers' self-efficacy have specific characteristics. These characteristics augment the teachers' sense of instructional efficacy which is then transferred through interaction with the students. Teachers who are efficacious work in schools that have:

- strong academic leadership,
- high academic standards with learning activities structured and conducted in ways to ensure mastery,
- firm belief in student capabilities,
- partnerships of mutual trust, understanding, and respect between administrators and each other,
- sensitivity and respect for learning and teaching differences,
- a collective sense of responsibility,
- structures that allow for problem solving versus assigning blame,
- systems that provide practical courses of action,
- power that is shared without undermining authority, and
- systems of communication designed to inform and educate parents. (Bandura, 1997)

School should be the place where all children learn the self regulatory skills needed to manage their learning, places where children develop both the knowledge and the problem solving skills needed for participating effectively in society. A strong sense of efficacy maintains the intrinsic interest and high levels of motivation students need for such academic accomplishment and eventual autonomy.

References

Bandura, Albert (1997). *Self Efficacy The Exercise of Control.* New York: W.H. Freemand and Company.

Conti-D'Antonio, M., Bertrando, R., & Eisenberger, J. (1998). *Supporting Students with Learning Needs in the Block.* Larchmont, NY: Eye On Education.

Costa, Arthur L. (1985). *Developing Minds: A Resource Book for Teaching Thinking.* Alexandria, VA: Association for Supervision and Curriculum Development.

Kouin, G. (1970). Discipline and group managment in classrooms. In J. Brophy, (1996). *Teaching Problem Students*, pp. 10–11. New York: Holt, Rinehart & Winston.

Landfried, Steven E. (1989). Enabling Underminds Responsibility in Students, *Education Leadership, 47,* 79–83.

Rimm, Sylvia B. (1997). An Underachievement Epidemic, *Education Leadership*, *54*, 18–22.

Sternberg, Robert (1988). *The Triarchic Mind: A New Theory of Human Intelligence*. New York: Viking Press.

2

INSTRUCTING FOR SELF-EFFICACY

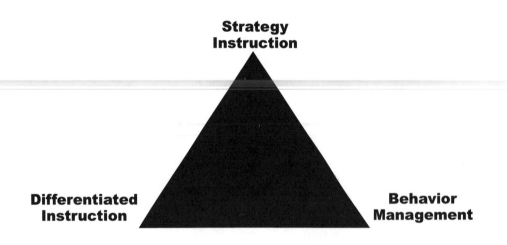

No Child Left Behind (NCLB) and Individuals with Disabilities Improvement Act (IDEA '04) has mandated that the progress of all students, including those with disabilities and learning problems is to the greatest extent possible the responsibility of general education teachers. IDEA '04 has also broadened the scope of the curriculum beyond content knowledge to include processes and progress. The politicians, parents, and teachers who supported the passing of IDEA '04 have reconfirmed the basic democratic nature, purpose, and benefits of public education:

♦ To support the development of a national identity among a diverse population

♦ To build the capacity for individuals to contribute individually and collectively to the economic well-being of the nation

♦ To create a literate citizenry that is capable of participating meaningfully and responsibly in a democratic society

♦ To provide a strong general knowledge base and the skills necessary to continue learning

Although the intentions of NCLB and IDEA '04 are laudable, the reality is that many general education and special education teachers are struggling with the new instructional role that has been thrust upon them. Special education teachers, many of whom spend most of their teaching time providing tutorial instruction, are struggling to redefine their purpose and to learn how to be successful with students who are being educated in the general curriculum. General education teachers, accustomed to delivering content, are now faced with educating students who have difficulty processing, representing, organizing, and retrieving information. If both groups of teachers are going to be successful, instruction must change, and a paradigm shift in what needs to be taught, as well as how a curriculum is taught, must occur.

A PARADIGM SHIFT

Consider the continuum of teacher views toward students and the actions taken by them based on those views shown in Figure 2.1. Educators' personal beliefs play a critical role in influencing student achievement and can be enabling or empowering, but not usually both. If students with learning needs are to be successful, teachers must make an effort to move their view of students toward the right on the continuum.

FIGURE 2.1. THE CONTINUUM OF TEACHER VIEWS FROM ENABLING TO EMPOWERING

Enabling ← ————————————————— → *Empowering*

Students "need" the special education teacher if they are to be successful	Students are capable of growth through short-term intervention and return to the mainstream
The goal is for students to pass courses with Cs or better	The goal is for students to share decision making and responsibility with the teacher
Students receive short-term subject area tutoring designed to pass the next evaluation	Students receive instruction in strategies that transfers into all areas of school and the real world
Students depend on the system or the teacher and will fail without them	Students can become independent and will need less support in the future
Students need protection and rescue from the demands of academia	Students need to reflect on their thinking or actions to affect positive change

The strategy instruction required to increase efficacy and achievement in students with learning needs is intense and time consuming (Hughes, 1999). It is much easier for teachers to engage in short-term "feel good" tutorials or to deliver "help" that borders on cheating when administering tests. This practice serves no one well because it has very little lasting impact on the student's current behavior and often ensures dependence on the people doing the "helping."

For special education teachers, the shift must be away from tutorial as the sole function of special education classes. Special education teachers must expand their job to include teaching their students the self-efficacy skills needed to be independent learners. While supporting students in their general education courses, special education teachers must teach their students to apply what they know consistently, persistently, and skillfully, especially when the going gets tough and the stakes are high (Bandura, 1997). Both special education and general education teachers need to recognize and respect the notion that children who have deficiencies need large amounts of persuasion and positive experiences to overcome doubts about their ability and capacities.

The shift for general education teachers must be toward delivering a curriculum that includes instruction in the skills necessary for self-direction. Content instruction alone no longer suffices. General education teachers need to analyze existing curriculum to determine what tasks are worth having students spend time on and think about as they integrate the national and state standards. In other words, they must determine what in their courses are worth remembering, understanding thoroughly, and transferring to other areas. To be most successful with the wide variety of learning needs and nontraditional learners in all classrooms, general education teachers must now include instruction in the processes and strategies needed for independence such as those outlined by Bandura (1997):

♦ Instruction in the skills needed for planning, organizing, and managing activities

♦ Instruction in the skills needed for enlisting help and resources at appropriate times

♦ Instruction in the skills needed for regulating one's own motivation and to sustain involvement in activities

♦ Instruction in the skills needed for applying metacognitive knowledge and strategies for task completion

♦ Instruction in the skills needed for acquisition of the knowledge and skill for managing the environment

Special education and the general education teachers need to cooperate to develop criteria that can be used to measure performance with the focus on proximal learning goals and progress rather than products alone. Both groups must also develop multiple ways for students to show what they know, can do, and understand as well as provide students with feedback that rewards and reinforces performance. All educators must also understand that intellectual self doubts often plague special education students and prevent them from putting enough effort into academic activities. (For more information on assessing student progress, see Chapter 4.)

DIFFERENTIATED INSTRUCTION

The mandate of inclusion means that teachers must differentiate instruction to optimize learning for all students. Differentiated Instruction, developed by Carol Ann Tomlinson (1999), is a highly effective instructional framework for meeting the needs of a wide variety of students. In a differentiated classroom, general education teachers recognize and accept that students learn in different ways and at different rates, have different interests and different talents, and bring different life experiences with them. They plan for student similarities and student differences by carefully identifying the essential concepts, principles, and skills of their curriculum and by carefully constructing rigorous, but engaging, instruction that promotes a high degree of self-efficacy.

Differentiating Instruction is the process of varying the content the students are learning, the activities the students are engaged in, or the products students produce. This differentiation is further extended by considering students' readiness to learn, their level of interest in the material being explored, or the students' learning style or intelligence strength preferences. Instead of teaching to the middle, teachers who use Differentiating Instruction design multiple paths to learning and multiple ways for students to show what they know, understand, and can do. Differentiating Instruction allows gifted students to accelerate through the course work or to work at a high level of abstraction. At the same time, students who struggle with academic demands find or are given appropriate entry points for learning. As a result of this differentiation, all students have the opportunity to learn as much and as deeply as they can without the anxiety of being bored because the task is too limiting or frustrated because the learning is too taxing.

Because students in a differentiated classroom are engaged in different tasks while learning the same objective, specific preparation may need to be done. Teachers can help prepare students for differentiation by paying specific attention to the following:

- ◆ Building Acceptance
  - Engage in class and team building
  - Use cooperative learning structures
  - Use flexible grouping
  - Develop a sense of community
  - Establish common learning goals
  - Plan for multiple intelligence and learning styles
- ◆ Establishing Safety and Order
  - Articulate classroom rules clearly
  - Keep materials organized and easily accessible
  - Explain expectations clearly
  - Build in a tolerance for error and questions
  - Create and deliver instructions carefully
  - Engage students in talking about procedures
- ◆ Planning for correction and instruction so that each student gains competence
  - Activate Prior Knowledge
  - Provide a way to "fill in" knowledge gaps
  - Acknowledge small and large successes
  - Validate responses
  - Provide a way for students to get help
  - Keep parents informed

♦ Placing a High Value on Learning
  • Be enthusiastic
  • Keep all activity and product requirements rigorous
  • Teach learning strategies specifically
  • Have kid-watching tools prepared
  • Include both summative and formative evaluations
  • Make expected outcomes explicit
  • Give students responsibility for their own learning

A pyramid planner (Figure 2.2, p. 22) can ensure that consideration is given to the critical components of instructional design. The teacher can identify how the facts, concepts, and generalizations will be differentiated on the left side of the pyramid planner. The activities or processes that the students will engage in to construct for meaning can be listed on the right side of the planner. The teacher might also choose to differentiate the ways in which the student will demonstrate what they know, understand, or are able to do in the section of the pyramid planner labeled Products. To maximize efficacy training, specific learning strategies need to be embedded into content-rich lessons. Finally, the teacher must plan for both summative and formative assessment. The formative assessments will guide and inform subsequent instruction, and the summative measures will indicate the content and processes the students have learned.

Carol Ann Tomlinson (1999, p. 2) said it best:

> These teachers believe that all students should be held to high standards. They work diligently to ensure that struggling, advanced, and in-between students think and work harder than they meant to; achieve more then they thought they could; and come to believe that learning involves effort, risk, and personal triumph. These teachers also work to ensure that each student consistently experiences the reality that success is likely to follow hard work.

STRATEGY INSTRUCTION

Although incorporating ways to select, use, and monitor strategies for learning benefits all students, it is critical for nontraditional learners. Students with learning needs require the techniques, principles, or routines that enable them to solve problems and complete tasks independently. Teachers need to make the instruction of learning strategies part of their instructional scope and sequence if they are to be successful with students with learning needs. These students will need instruction in choosing the correct strategies, practice in applying the strategies, and reminders and reinforcements for exercising better control over academic tasks by using the strategies. The goal must be to enhance the students' belief in their self-efficacy, the ability to exercise control over academic progress. A new function of special education teachers is to work

**FIGURE 2.2. A GRAPHIC ORGANIZER FOR
DIFFERENTIATING INSTRUCTION[1]**

Pyramid Planner for Differentiating Instruction

Content (differentiated by Ⓡ I P ?)   **Activities** (differentiated by Ⓡ I P ?):

What SOME will learn: Use the algorithm (A=LxW) to find area	<u>Concrete—Using a sq. unit to find the area</u> <u>of various objects in the room.</u> <u>Representative—Create a visual represent-</u> <u>ation to prove a given # sentence.</u> <u>Abstract—Infer the formula from a graphic</u> <u>representation</u>

Products (differentiated by RⒾP ?):

What MOST students will learn: Use a graphic to explain the formula for area	<u>Construct an illustration using polygons,</u> <u>angles & area.</u> <u>Choose from: alien, underwater, sea animal,</u> <u>room in a house</u>

What ALL students should learn: Count area in sq. units Identify angles: acute, obtuse & right angle Identify polygons and their properties	<u>Learning Strategies</u> <u>Math attack</u> <u>Think along</u> <u>Requesting help</u>

Teaching Strategies: <u>Whole class and small Group (cooperative Learning budies)</u>
Assessment: <u>Observation on using Skills checklist, rubric for product</u>

---

1 For more information on the Learning Strategies mentioned below, see Appendix I: Strategies. A reproducible copy of the Pyramid Planner is located in Appendix II: Forms.

cooperatively with the general education teacher to identify those strategies that are critical for the student to meet the demands of the curriculum.

Special education teachers must recognize that students with learning needs will be more successful if the focus of support class is the explicit, structured teaching of learning strategies. The student response in Figure 2.3 illustrates that students also recognize the value of strategy instructions.

FIGURE 2.3. A STUDENT CHOOSES STRATEGY INSTRUCTION

In a recent discussion with Mrs. Conti-D'Antonio I made the decision to keep the every other day scheduling. This program is working well for me so far. My grades have improved a little bit and I feel more confident about school. Maybe in a future marking period I could maybe lessen my time and study more independently but for now I would like learn some more study skills and improve my grades up into the A and B range.

Because strategy instruction is intense and time-consuming, students need to know the rationale for the strategies they are being asked to use (Hughes, 1999). When a strategy has been taught to a student, the strategy must be maintained, practiced, and reflected on until it has become a part of the student's standard operating procedure. This requires substantially less time tutoring and much more time doing the following:

- ◆ Using diagnostic teaching—Being aware of the strategies the students are using, suggesting additional steps, teaching more efficient methods, making procedural corrections, or giving compliments
- ◆ Encouraging active learning—Requiring more prereading, prewriting, cooperative learning than the completing of homework
- ◆ Interrupting homework to provide as much practice and review of the strategies as possible—placing equal importance on process and product
- ◆ Pointing out and encouraging continued use and generalization of strategies
- ◆ Emphasizing the importance of automaticity of the strategies and basic skills as time savers
- ◆ Teaching students to monitor their own progress as they use the strategies—metacognitive awareness as well as automaticity are necessary for efficacy
- ◆ Reflecting on the success and the limitations of their strategies

Support teachers should be prepared to use a step-by-step approach to structure the initial steps in teaching a cognitive strategy. The process, Three Steps to Teaching Procedures, detailed by Harry and Rosemary Wong in *The First Day of School* (1998), is an ideal model.

1. **Explain.** State, explain, model, and demonstrate the procedure.

   Define the procedure in concrete terms.

   Demonstrate the procedures; don't just tell.

   Demonstrate a complex procedure step by step.

2. **Rehearse.** Rehearse and practice the procedure.

   Practice, step by step, under supervision and check for accuracy.

   Repeat the procedure until it seems routine.

3. **Reinforce.** Reteach, rehearse, practice, and reinforce the procedure until it is habit.

   Assess the automaticity and correctness of the procedure.

   Reteach any steps that are incorrect or unacceptable.

   Give corrective feedback.

   Praise the student when correction is made.

Because most of the lessons in a learning support classroom are individual, the best instruction occurs in short, less than 10-minute discussions with a student. The more the lesson can be compacted, the more powerful the message. The following four-step sequence is an effective model.

1. In 30 seconds or less, describe the issue. Use a Positive-Negative-Positive Feedback with "I message" format and end with a question. The teacher says, "You have such great potential and I am very concerned about your F in English. I would like to support you in your effort to get that grade up to passing. Can we plan together?"

2. Spend the next minute mirroring reality for the student. Provide an honest (but not brutal) overview of what has caused the problem. Do not use guilt or blame. Simply state the causes matter-of-factly and end with a question. The teacher says, "You have an F because you did not turn in the last three assignments. Can you share with me why you're are not doing the work?"

3. After listening to the student's explanation, spend the next two or three minutes teaching a strategy that will provide a solution for the student's dilemma. Make sure the strategy fits the subject and the student's learning style and will solve the problem if the student uses it. End with a question that asks for the student's commitment. The teacher says, "I have a suggestion for you. I want you to try to

use Hard to Easy for the next English assignment. This is what you need to do to use that strategy....Are you willing to try this for the next assignment?"

4. In 30 seconds or less, describe the payoff for the student (or ask the student to describe the payoff). The teacher says, "What will you have to give up to do this? What will you get?" Be positive, upbeat, and enthusiastic. Describe how the student will feel about the benefits of the strategy.

Because students with learning needs struggle to organize multiple tasks, both general teachers and special education teachers need to impose a "framework" that incorporates multiple strategies and give students enough guided practice in using the framework so that it becomes internalized and routine. Because students with learning needs do not spontaneously structure tasks and have difficulty activating specific strategies at appropriate times (Meltzer, 1993), substrategies and routines may also need to be taught. More information about specific strategies can be found in Appendix I. Academic progress is enhanced by instructional time devoted to teaching students how to develop solid, efficient learning plans. Time after completion of the activity for students to reflect on the effectiveness of their plans is also necessary.

One such framework is the Objective Test-Taking Cycle shown in Figure 2.4. The steps in the Objective Test-Taking Cycle provide visual, concrete guides to the multiple tasks needed to prepare for a test. The Cycle requires students to define how they will find and organize information; how they will shift from one strategy to the next and back again, if necessary; how they will monitor and check on their levels of readiness; and how they will evaluate the effectiveness of their chosen strategies when the test has been completed. Having a concrete model of the test preparation steps (Figure 2.5, p. 28) raises the level of awareness of the usefulness of strategies and illustrates the complex nature of test preparation.

A second framework that is important for students with learning needs involves the multiple mental tasks and skills that are needed to acquire information from written material. The process of extracting meaning from text combines several complex skills including reading comprehension, identifying key information and separating that information from examples and explanations, paraphrasing, and organizing information. The following framework is often called SQRRR, but Muscle Reading, a name coined by David Ellis (1991), is more descriptive of the effort needed to dig the key information from most texts and from some literature.

This framework (Figure 2.6, p. 29) gives a student a series of substrategies for extracting knowledge and information from extended passages in textbooks. This system works especially well for social studies and science texts because embedded language and dense information are the norm. At first, the system may seem awkward and cumbersome, and it takes time to learn and master. The payoff is a deeper understanding of written information, substantially less time rereading material, and a quality study guide to use in test preparation. If students are engaged in research, the same framework yields the notes needed to extract, organize, and synthesize the information needed to complete the project.

An additional framework involves using Graphic Organizers (Figure 2.7, p. 30) to coordinate the multiple tasks and skills needed to develop information-processing skills, demonstrate understanding of information, and organize written expression. The goal is to do what Edwin S. Ellis (1997) calls "Water Up" the curriculum so that all students have the effective and efficient strategies needed for meaningful learning. These graphic organizers allow students to construct knowledge instead of simply memorizing isolated facts. They allow students to understand the content by clarifying details and joining the details into meaningful wholes. They also make it possible for students to see how information falls into connected patterns and how the materials they are learning connects to their prior knowledge and experiences. Using the graphic organizers encourages elaboration in thought and writing and makes abstract information more concrete.

The final framework (Figure 2.8, p. 31) gives students a way to approach and organize the strategies needed for the successful completion of homework. This framework can be used to organize the strategies and the mental mind-set a student needs to complete the assigned work independently. Routinely using the Study Planner framework during class provides the guided practice in using the multiple tasks required for organizing time, materials, and attention students need on their journey to independence. General education teachers can also use the framework whenever their students are required to plan and work for a sustained period of time.

An additional benefit of the Study Planner is the opportunity it provides for the collection and recording of data about a student's progress toward self-efficacious behavior (see Figure 2.9, p. 32). Information noted on the Study Planner can guide instruction, provide a rich source of information for parent conferences, and form longitudinal study of a student's progress. For more information on working with parents and collecting data on student progress, see Chapters 4 and 5.

CLASSROOM MANAGEMENT

To be most effective, both Differentiated Instruction and Strategy Instruction should be conducted in classrooms where an efficacious environment has been established by teachers who have good behavior-management skills (Bandura, 1997). This environment is especially critical for nontraditional learners, many of whom act impulsively and have difficulty reading subtle social and environmental cues. Students who have learning needs require efficacious teachers who endorse high standards, backing them up with strong management

(Text continues on page 32.)

FIGURE 2.4. THE OBJECTIVE TEST-TAKING CYCLE[2]

Steps	*Possible Strategies*
❶ Set a Goal: Target a grade / Establish a time frame / Commit to strategies	Conferencing Journalizing Goal Pyramid / I Can Goal Visualization
❷ Identify Key Information	Graphic Organizer Cued Notes 3-Fold Page / Clustering Highlighting Cornell Notes / Math Assault Flashcards Post-Its / Color Coding Skimming Muscle Reading
❸ Memorize	Walk About Do & Redo Memory Webbing / Oral Research Peer Teacher Write then Read / Acronym Splashdown Key Word Pictures
❹ Check Memory: Recall the information / Keep track of # correct / Calculate your score	Practice Test Study Partner 3-Fold Page / Oral Retrieval Splashdown Flashcards / Walk About Computer Drill Cover & Recite
❺ Adjust Goal	Reward Yourself Goal Setting Accepting Feedback
❻ Repeat Steps 2, 3, 4	I will repeat: 1 2 3 4 5 times
❼ Take the Test	Visualization Splashdown Oral Retrieval / Eliminating Options Steal It Cued Notes / Easy to Hard Using Margins / Chairs in Place
❽ Reflect on Performance	Reward Yourself Conclusions I Can / Requesting Help Consequences / Test Critique
❾ Adjust Strategies	Responding to Persuasion Responding to Help / Decision Making Requesting Help
❿ Repeat the Cycle	Get a new Objective Test-Taking Cycle and begin preparing for the next test.

2 For more information on many of the strategies listed in the Objective Test-Taking Cycle, see Appendix I: Strategies. A reproducible copy of the Objective Test Taking Cycle is found in Appendix II: Forms.

FIGURE 2.5. A STUDENT USES A FRAMEWORK FOR CHOOSING, ORGANIZING, AND USING THE MULTIPLE STRATEGIES NEEDED FOR TEST PREPARATION[3]

Objective Test Preparation Planner

STEP	*STRATEGIES*
	<u>Economics</u>
1. Set a Goal	1. What grade are you willing to work for?
	<u>A</u>
2. Identify the Key Information	2. How will you separate out the facts that will be on the test?
	<u>Cornell notes</u>
3. Memorize the Information	3. How will you get the information into long-term memory?
	<u>Oral Rehearsal</u>
4. Check Memory	4. How will you find out if the facts are really in your memory and you can get them out of memory?
	<u>Oral Quiz (partner)</u>
5. Adjust Target Grade	5. How will you know if you can reach your original goal?
	<u>By how much I know</u>
6. Repeat Steps 3 to 5	6. How many times will you repeat Steps 3, 4, and 5 before the test?
	<u>3 times, 1 each day before test</u>
7. Take Test	7. What strategies will you use during the test?
	<u>Stop and Think, Oral retrieval, Eliminate opt.</u>
8. Critique Test Performance	8. How will you figure out what went right and what went wrong?
	<u>By the Grade I received and what ?'s I misse.</u>
9. Adjust Strategies	9. How will you prepare for your next test?
	<u>The same way if it worked</u>
10. Repeat the cycle	

---

3 For copies of the strategies mentioned by the student and a reproducible copy of the Objective Test Planner, see Appendix I: Strategies and Appendix II: Forms.

FIGURE 2.6. THE MUSCLE READING FRAMEWORK[4]

Phase	Steps	Possible Strategies
Phase I Before you read (5 to 15 minutes)	1. **Preview**—Flip through the pages looking at section headings, picture captions, bold words. 2. **Warm-up**—Read the chapter review and the vocabulary list, identifying what you know. 3. **Notice**—Determine how the text is organized. 4. **Choose**—Select a note-taking strategy. 5. **Question**—Turn chapter headings and section titles into questions.	Prior Knowledge Request Help Decision Making Paraphrasing Study Partner
Phase II Reading & Writing (10 to 30 minutes)	1. **Read**—Use your questions to keep your focus and read aloud when your mind wanders. 2. **Visualize**—Picture the material in your mind. 3. **Take Notes**—Use the note-taking strategy selected. 4. **Answer**—Write the answers to the questions you asked yourself in the prereading phase. 5. **Expand**—Add details to your notes from class discussion and lectures. 6. **Predict**—Check your notes against what you think will be on the test. 7. **Question**—Write questions about what you don't understand and ask about those points in class.	Key Points Key Word Picture Graphic Organizer Post-Its Process 3-Fold Page Cornell Notes Outline Highlighting Flashcards Request Help

4 For descriptions of many of the strategies listed in the Muscle Reading Framework, see Appendix I: Strategies. A reproducible bookmark for students to use as a guide and reminder can be found in Appendix II: Forms.

Phase	Steps	Possible Strategies
Phase III After you read (5 to 10 minutes)	1. **Recite**—Talk to yourself about what you have learned, explaining as much as you can about each key point. 2. **Review**—Look at your notes within 24 hours of reading the material and fill in anything that you didn't understand. 3. **Check**—Practice retrieval to see what is already in your memory and what isn't. 4. **Review Again**—Review your notes once a day for about 5 minutes, reciting the more complicated information.	Oral Rehearsal Key Points Practice Test Oral Retrieval Cover & Recite Study Partner Do & Redo

FIGURE 2.7. GRAPHIC ORGANIZERS[5]

Function	Graphic Organizers
Construct Knowledge	Semantic Maps including Webs Debate Organizers
Clarifying/Connecting Details	Core Planning Charts Taba Charts Concept Clarifiers
Recognizing Patterns	Action-Reaction Charts Problem-Solving Structures Cause & Effect Diagrams
Elaboration	Multiparagraph Organizers

5 Two excellent sources of graphic organizers are Black, H., and Black, S. (1990), Book 1 and Book 2—Organizing Thinking: Graphic Organizers, Pacific Grove, CA: Midwest Publications, and Edwin Ellis (1999), Using Graphic Organizers to Make Sense of the Curriculum, Tuscaloosa, AL: Masterminds.

**FIGURE 2.8. A FRAMEWORK FOR LEARNING
TIME MANAGEMENT AND TASK COMPLETION[6]**

The Study Planner

Steps and Strategies	*The Plan*	
Before studying: Hard to Easy Assignment Tracking Materials Management Personal Checklists Chairs in Place Goal Visualization	I **organize** myself during the first 5 minutes by making a plan that clearly identifies my goal, subject, assignment, and strategy. **Goal:** _____ **Subject:** _____ **Assignment:** _____ **Strategy:** _____ I take responsibility for my **materials** by gathering all the supplies and equipment I need to complete the work I plan before I began.	
During the study session: Relax with Black Requesting Help Muscle Reading Stop and Think (Plus strategies specific to homework assignments)	I managed my **time** by beginning work at the time I have chosen. I show **commitment** by working the entire time I had planned, asking for assistance when I need information or instruction to complete my planned work. I actively participate in my own education by **completing** the work I planned so that I can achieve the goals I have established. I put myself back **on task** when distracted.	
After the study session: Rate yourself using the following key: I Can Accepting Feedback Smoke and Mirrors Stop and Think	4 = Mastered	I do this automatically. It is part of my school behavior.
	3 = Good	Even though I know this would help me be more successful, I still need to be reminded. I don't do this automatically.
	2 = Needs Work	I know I should do this, but I often need to be reminded. I only do this when an adult suggests this or reminds me that it needs to be done.
	1 = Not Yet	I only did this because I was forced to or because I was being watched.
	0 = Refuse	I refused to do this or I did not think this is necessary for me.

6 For descriptions of many of the strategies listed on the Study Planner, see Appendix I: Strategies. A reproducible copy of the Study Planner can be found in Appendix II: Forms.

**FIGURE 2.9. A STUDENT PLANS FOR A 40-MINUTE CLASS AND
A TEACHER RECORDS INFORMATION OF EFFICACIOUS BEHAVIOR[7]**

Date <u>11/23</u> **Period** <u>5</u> **Teacher** <u>E</u>   **SCORING:**   **Student**   **Teacher**

Goal: <u>all goals</u>   1. Organize   <u>4</u>   <u>4</u>

                                                   2. Responsibility   <u>4</u>   __

Subject: <u>all subjects</u>   3. Materials   <u>4</u>   __

Assignment: <u>Where are you now</u>   4. Commitment   <u>4</u>   __

                                                   5. Completing   <u>4</u>   __

Strategy: <u>Conferencing</u>   6. Time   <u>4</u>   __

                                                   7. Feedback   <u>4</u>   __

Assignment: _____   8. On Task   <u>4</u>   __

Strategy: _____   9. Communicate   <u>4</u>   __

                                                              TOTAL: <u>100</u>

COMMENTS: <u>Complete goal & reflection & cleaned portfolios—</u>
                 <u>Said he didn't do homework because he believed it was "too hard"</u>

INSTRUCTION: Requesting Help

---

skills, and who provide, or at least cooperate with, support systems that aid mastery, and who believe that difficult students are teachable.

Good managers, those teachers who establish, maintain, and restore conditions that promote learning, have specific characteristics (Kounin, 1970). First, these teachers prevent disruption from occurring by providing effective environments and monitoring student behavior. Good managers do this by establishing standard operating procedures during the first weeks of school and then consistently maintain those procedures throughout the year. They establish routines quickly and clearly, and then monitor for compliance. Behaviors such as voice levels as well as rules about when to sharpen pencils and how to ask questions are observed, and consequences are consistently enforced.

Second, effective managers recognize and reward good behavior more often than they react to bad behavior. When it becomes necessary to punish, they do so with sadness and regret as though punishment is an unfortunate, necessary consequence of students' misbehavior but something that a student could avoid in the future if they wanted to do so. Teachers with strong instructional ef-

---

7 For more details on the strategies Conferencing and Requesting Help, see Appendix I: Strategies. For a reproducible copy of the study planner, see Appendix II: Forms.

ficacy tend to rely on persuasion instead of punitive measures and work toward the development of students' academic self-directedness.

Third, good managers minimize disruption by knowing when transitions will be difficult for students and by planning how to manage those transition times. They are keenly aware of who sits where and why. They plan the physical environment of their classroom so that it is most conducive to learning. They think through traffic patterns, determine where supplies will be kept so that traffic to and from those supplies is least disruptive, and they attend promptly to house-keeping chores. They recognize that most classroom disruptions can be prevented by diligently providing instruction that is rigorous, varied, and meets the needs of a wide variety of learners.

Kounin (1970) also identified four key behaviors that good managers use:

1. **With-It-Ness**—Continuously scanning the classroom, being aware of what is happening in all parts of the classroom, and intervening quickly and accurately before behaviors become disruptive by recognizing and responding to triggers.

2. **Overlapping**—Doing three or more things at once: responding to individual needs while sustaining the groups activities through the use of proximity, eye contact, or visual cues.

3. **Momentum & Continuity**—Developing compelling, well-paced lessons that are more attractive than the distractors.

4. **Challenge & Variety**—Maintaining effort through rigor and interest through differentiation.

Finally, good managers are aware that students with learning needs are not all alike and that different needs require different solutions. They are also aware that they do not have as much control over a student's behavior as they have over their own and that managing their own behavior will have a dramatic effect on the behavior of their students. The matrix in Figure 2.10 (pp. 34–38) is partially based on the work of Jere Brophy (1996) and Lynn Meltzer (1992) and identifies the teacher behavior that is most effective with individual problem types and the specific strategies that are most successful. Many of the strategies mentioned in the matrix can be found in the Appendix I: Strategies.

The goal of efficacious instruction should be the goal of inclusive schools —to teach the student the self-regulatory capabilities that enable the student to be reflective learners, capable of ongoing growth and persistence in the face of challenges.

(Text continues on page 38.)

FIGURE 2.10. A LIST OF PROBLEM TYPES, INDICATORS FOR ACCURATE IDENTIFICATION, APPROPRIATE TEACHER BEHAVIORS, AND STRATEGIES THAT MAY NEED TO BE TAUGHT[8]

Problem Student Type	Indicators	Teacher Behavior	Student Strategies
Flexibility disabilities: These children have difficulty shifting flexibly among different approaches. They may struggle to prioritize and to focus on salient details.	1. Difficulty adjusting to new teachers, situations 2. Talk around issues, cannot summarize 3. Poor study skills 4. Low reading comprehension	1. Scaffolding techniques 2. Clearly identify salient attributes of work 3. Sequenced, direct teaching of strategies 4. Environmental/ physical cues for expected behavior	1. Strategies for rapid retrieval 2. Self-reflection strategies 3. Study routines: Math Assault, 5-day test prep, Muscle Reading 4. Summarizing strategies
Processing disabilities: These children process information slowly or in unique ways. They may be disorganized or use different processing routes to organize information. They show extremely strong learning style preference for one modality.	1. Discrepancies between class and test performance 2. Difficulty with timed tasks 3. Difficulty following directions 4. Written work, book bags are messy and disorganized 5. Often unprepared 6. Struggles to remember	1. Spiral or scaffolding instruction 2. Transfer cues 3. Require organization but not *one* method 4. Allow for extended time to organize, copy, process information	1. Semantic mapping, graphic organizers 2. Memorization strategies 3. Strategies that use strengths and bypass weaknesses 4. Self-checking strategies

---

8 For descriptions of many of the strategies listed in this matrix, see Appendix I: Strategies.

Problem Student Type	Indicators	Teacher Behavior	Student Strategies
Efficiency disabilities: These children do not finish assigned work. They do not monitor their work habits. They have difficulty coordinating the tasks needed to learn. They do not plan or check and begin work impulsively.	1. Slow to master strategies 2. Strong conceptual and reasoning skills 3. Cling to old habits 4. Inconsistent 5. "Careless" errors 6. "Lost" work	1. Coordinate multiple processes for student 2. Pace strategies used in close succession or simultaneously 3. Enforce consequences and reflect on causes	1. Organizational strategies 2. Planning and self-checking strategies 3. Goal setting and achievement 4. Strategies for directed attention (rubrics, ✔lists) 5. Bypass strategies and devices—calculator, referenced notes
Distractible: These children have short attention spans. They are unable to sustain attention and concentration. They are easily distracted by sounds, sights, movement.	1. Difficulty adjusting to change and transitions 2. Rarely completes tasks 3. Easily pulled off task 4. Moves or talks at inappropriate times	1. Environmental and instructional support 2. Reduce demands for sustained attention 3. Proximity and eye contact	1. Strategy to monitor and control attention—grade and assignment tracking, cross off as you go, attention tapes 2. Material and time management strategies 3. Carrels, behavior ✔lists
Low Achiever: These children have difficulty, even though they may be willing to work. Their problem is low potential or lack of readiness rather than poor motivation.	1. Difficulty following directions 2. Difficulty completing work 3. Poor retention 4. Progresses slowly 5. Poor abstract reasoning	1. Extra time, repetition 2. Place a high value on working hard, not happiness 3. Effort and progress are required 4. Work is acceptable as long as students apply themselves and are making progress in the general curriculum	1. Bypass strategies and devices—calculators, graphic organizers, spell checkers, guided notes, editing partners 2. Strategy more important than content—Muscle Reading, positive self talk, requesting help 3. Realistic self-assessment 4. Charting progress

Problem Student Type	Indicators	Teacher Behavior	Student Strategies
Defiant: These children resist authority and engage in power struggles with teacher. They want to have their way and not be told what to do.	1. Resists verbally—"You can't make me." 2. Derogatory statements about teacher to others 3. Resists nonverbally—looks away, frowns, laughs at inappropriate times, mimics teacher, deliberately does what the teacher says not to do	1. Ignore and avoid as much as possible 2. No powerful responses 3. Functional relationship 4. Environmental engineering	1. Professional counseling 2. Negotiated contracts 3. Strategies for responding to others
Passive-Aggressive: These children express opposition and resistance but not directly. Hard to tell if the resistance is deliberate. Often misdiagnosed as immature or attention seeking. Miscellaneous in form but exasperating in effect.	1. Subtly oppositional and stubborn 2. Controlling, borderline compliance with rules 3. Damages property—writes on desks, mars books 4. Disrupts surreptitiously 5. Drags feet	1. Recognize accurately, follow up with strategies 2. Offer support but refrain from doing for 3. Recognize anger but don't overreact to it	1. Problem-solving and problem-investigation strategies 2. Efficacious strategies—Requesting Help, Following Directions 3. Socialization strategies—Accepting Feedback, Conferencing
Immature: These children have poorly developed emotional stability, self-control, self-care abilities, and social skills.	1. Exhibits behavior associated with much younger children 2. Cries easily 3. Loses belongings 4. Frequently helpless, incompetent, and/or dependent	1. Emotional support but not low expectations 2. Cuing 3. Value on behavior changes	1. Self-determination strategies — Responding to Persuasion 2. Self-reflection strategies 3. Problem-solving strategies

Problem Student Type	Indicators	Teacher Behavior	Student Strategies
Failure Syndrome: These children are convinced that they cannot do the work. They often avoid starting or give up easily. They expect to fail, even after succeeding.	1. Easily frustrated 2. Give up easily 3. Says, "I can't do this."	1. Negotiated agreements 2. Specific proximal goals 3. Feedback stressing success 4. Efficacy training	1. Contracting 2. Goal setting with reflection 3. Coping strategies —test taking, memorizing, time management 4. Self-determination strategies— I Can, positive self-talk
Hostile-Aggressive: These children express hostility through direct, intense behaviors. They are not easily controlled.	1. Intimidates/ threatens 2. Hits, damages property 3. Antagonizes, hostile 4. Easily angered	1. Avoid engage-ment 2. Enforce limits and consequences 3. Positive relationships	1. Professional help 2. Behavior management 3. Socialization strategies— accepting feedback, conferencing 4. Self-control strategies— dealing with frustration, managing anger
Peer rejected: These children seek peer interaction and acceptance but are rejected, ignored, or excluded.	1. Forced to work, play alone 2. Lack social skills 3. Picked on or teased	1. Positive group identity 2. Classroom as a learning community 3. "We…" statements	1. Socialization training 2. Strategies that target the undesirable trait
Shy-withdrawn: These children avoid personal interaction, are quiet and unobtrusive, and do not respond well to others.	1. Quiet and sober 2. Does not initiate or volunteer 3. Does not call attention to self	1. Expect slow change 2. Comfortable, secure classroom 3. Indirect pressure to change— invitation and encouragement 4. Cuing, shaping behavior 5. Environment engineering	1. Self-concept support—I can, eye contact. 2. Group projects 3. Study partners— Peer note takers, editing partners 4. Attention control strategies

Problem Student Type	Indicators	Teacher Behavior	Student Strategies
Perfectionist: These children are unduly anxious about making mistakes. Their self-imposed standards are unrealistically high, so that they are never satisfied with their work even when they should be.	1. Work must be perfect 2. Fearful/ frustrated with the quality of the work 3. Holds back from class participation	1. Understanding, approval, and empathy 2. Honor motivation 3. Offer support to maximize achievement	1. Goal setting 2. Self-assessment 3. Diagnostic thinking—rubric for success 4. Realistic feedback
Underachiever: These children do a minimum to just "get by." They do not value schoolwork.	1. Indifferent 2. Minimum work output 3. Not challenged by school work, poorly motivated	1. Realistic skill assessment 2. Value education, learning 3. Confrontive, persuasive 4. Empowering, enthusiastic	1. Establish purpose 2. Goal achievement 3. Monitor comprehension—paraphrasing, predicting 4. Strategies for all subjects and reflection on their use

REFERENCES

Bandura, A. (1997). *Self-Efficacy: The Exercise of Control*. New York: W.H. Freeman.

Barkley, R. (1990). *Attention Deficit-Hyperactivity Disorder: A Handbook for Diagnosis and Treatment*. New York: Guilford Press.

Black, H., & Black, S. (1990). *Book II—Organizing Thinking: Graphic Organizers*. Pacific Grove, CA: Midwest Publications.

Brophy, J. (1996). *Teaching Problem Students*. New York: Guilford Press.

Cawalti, G. (Ed.) (1995). *Handbook of Research on Improving Student Achievement*. Arlington, VA: Educational Research Service.

Choate, J. S. (1993). *Successful Mainstreaming: Proven Ways to Detect and Correct Special Needs*. Boston: Allyn and Bacon.

Conti-D'Antonio, M., Bertrando, R., & Eisenberger, J. (1998). *Supporting Students with Learning Needs in the Block*, Larchmont, NY: Eye On Education.

Costa, A. L. (1990). *The School as Home for the Mind*. Palatine, IL: Skylight Publishing.

Dawson, P. (1994, June). Homework survival guide. *Communique, 22* (8).

Deschler, D. D., & Schumaker, J. B. (1984). Learning strategies: An instructional alternative for low achieving adolescents. *Exceptional Children, 52*, 583–590.

DuPaul, G., & Stoner, G. (1994). *ADHD in the Schools: Assessment and Intervention Strategies*. New York: Guilford Press.

Ellis, D. B. (1991). *Becoming a Master Student*. Rapid City, SD: College Survival.

Ellis, E. S. (1991). An instrumental model for teaching learning strategies. *Focus on Exceptional Children, 23*, 1–24.

Ellis, E. S. (1997). Watering up the curriculum for adolescents with learning disabilities. *Remedial and Special Education, 18*, 326–346.

Ellis, E. S. (1999). *Using Graphic Organizers to Make Sense of the Curriculum*. Tuscaloosa, AL: Masterminds.

Gaskins, E., & Elliot, T. (1991). *Implementing Cognitive Strategy Training Across the School*. Philadelphia, PA: Brookline Books.

Hallowell, E., & Ratey, J. (1995). *Answers to Distraction*. New York: Pantheon Books.

Hughes, C. (1999, Spring). Helping adolescents with learning disabilities become strategic learners. *Bridges, Research into Practice*. State College, PA: Penn State.

Kounin, G. (1970). Discipline and group management in classrooms. In Brophy, J. (Ed.) (1996), *Teaching Problem Students* (pp. 10–11). New York: Holt, Rinehart & Winston.

Landfried, S. E. (1989). "Enabling" undermines responsibility in students. *Education Leadership, 47*, 61–65.

Levine, M. (1993). *All Kinds of Minds*. Cambridge, MA: EPS.

Meltzer, L. (1992). *Strategy Use in Students with Learning Disabilities: The Challenge of Assessment, Strategy Assessment and Instruction for Students with Learning Disabilities: From Theory to Practice*. Austin, TX: Pro-Ed.

Meltzer, L. (Ed.) (1993). *Strategy Assessment and Instruction for Students with Learning Disabilities—From Theory to Practice*. Austin, TX: Pro-Ed.

Nadeau, K., Dixon, E., & Biggs, S. (1993). *School Strategies for ADD Teens*. Chesapeake, MD: Psychological Publications.

Perrone, V. (1994). How to engage students in learning. *Educational Leadership, 51*, 11–13.

Rimm, S. (1997, April). An underachievement epidemic. *Education Leadership, 54*(7), 19–22.

Tomlinson, C. A. (1999). *The Differentiated Classroom, Responding to the Needs of All Learners*. Alexandria, VA: Association for Supervision and Curriculum Development.

Udvari-Solner, A., & Thousand, J. S. (1995). Promising practices that foster inclusive education. In Villa, R. A., & Thousand, J. S. (Eds.), *Creating an Inclusive School* (pp. 110–124). Alexandria, VA: Association for Supervision and Curriculum Development.

Wiggins, G. (1993). Standards, not standardization. *Educational Leadership, 48*, 18–25.

Wiggins, G., & McTaig, J. (1998). *Understanding by Design*. Alexandria, VA: Association for Supervision and Curriculum Development.

Wong, H., & Wong, R. (1998). *The First Day of School*. Mountainview, CA: Harry K. Wong.

3

LEARNING TO LEARN— EXERCISES THAT PROMOTE EFFICACY

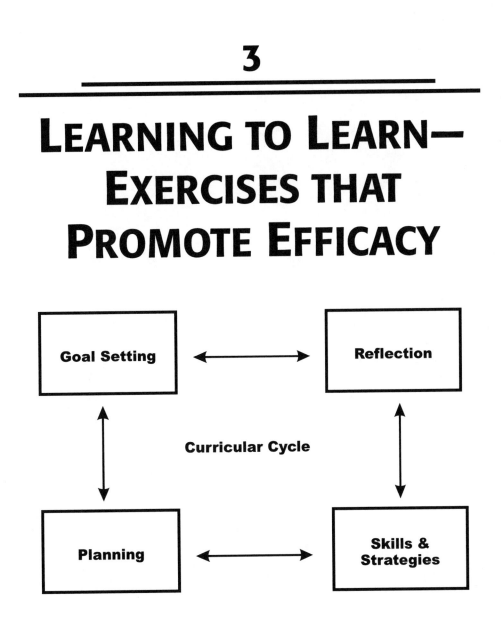

Responsible inclusion requires a continuum of service for students with learning needs. The majority of these students are well served through general education classes with appropriate accommodations and modifications. However, some students require cooperative planning between the special education support teacher and the content teacher to differentiate instruction and build in multiple ways for all students to learn and show what they know, understand, and can do. Other students need classes that are both cooperatively planned and taught so that they can learn. Still other students have learning needs that are unique enough that they must be taught how to face the gaps in their knowledge, skills, and competencies and be given experience with guided practice in the skills necessary to manage school and life outside of school.

Support teachers will still need to teach some students in small groups outside the content classroom to meet their unique needs. However, the primary focus of these groups can no longer be tutorial. If students are to succeed in inclusive schools and enter society as autonomous adults, the support teachers must see their role as teaching for self-efficacy and independence. While working in the content area in which the student is deficient, support teachers and general education teachers must design exercises and tasks that teach students to regulate their motivation and study environment, to control their learning and memory strategies, and to be reflective. These instructional exercises should bolster the students' beliefs in their academic efficacy and build the skills needed for them to fulfill their aspirations. The students should be guided, given feedback, and reinforced positively as they persistently practice the application of skills and strategies in the face of difficulties, stressors, and competing social attractions.

Although many of the following exercises can be performed efficiently in the intimacy of a learning support classroom, most can easily be merged into the routine of a general education course. Each is part of a recursive pattern of goal setting, planning, metacognitive use of strategies, and reflection.

Within the recursive pattern of goal setting, planning, metacognitive use of strategies, and reflection, students will need instruction and guided practice to select and structure their own academic environment. To exercise self-efficacious behaviors, students need to develop the skills to establish a consistent study environment and to mobilize and sustain motivation through goal activation. These include the skill to:

- Establish and achieve proximal goals;
- Maintain regular times and regular places of study;
- Recognize and control the activities that interfere with the completion of academic tasks;
- Practice temporary self-denial when faced with attractive alternatives to study;
- Reflect on and choose to improve academic skills.

Students also need exercises designed to give them instruction and practice in establishing control over their learning and memory. Through this series of exercises, students strengthen their ability to select appropriate study strategies when they need to construct for meaning and manage information. These include the skill to:

- Select strategies for condensing, paraphrasing, and synthesizing information to construct for meaning;
- Identify and record key information from discussion, lecture, and texts;
- Organize information into recallable chunks;
- Rehearse information in preparation of summative tests;
- Reflect on the use of and effectiveness of strategies.

Finally, students need instruction and guided practice in planning for transition from one school level to the next, and, ultimately, to college or work. These skills include the ability to request appropriate accommodations and to make decisions based on factual information as well as the skill to:

- Know and use information about learning styles and multiple intelligence;
- Know, request, and use appropriate accommodations;
- Explore, discuss, and relate current skill levels to the next level of school and life;
- Reflect on and choose to improve metacognitive skills and strategies.

GOAL SETTING

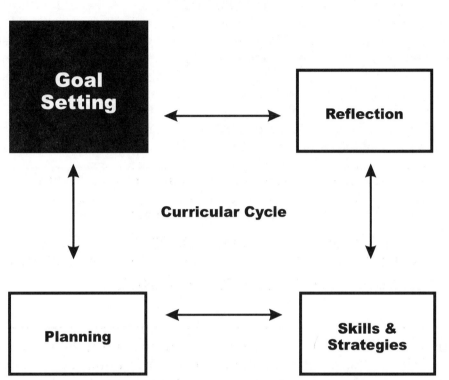

There are various entry points within the recursive pattern of Goal Setting, Planning, metacognitive uses of Strategies, and Reflection. Teachers should decide the best entry points for instruction based on the needs of the student and the demands of the general curriculum. Recognizing where to enter this recursive cycle, and the direction in which to move through the cycle, requires teachers to identify opportunities for instruction. These opportunities become apparent during liaison meetings, cooperative planning meetings, transition planning, and observations of the students. Curriculum artifacts and teacher knowledge of the general curriculum can provide additional data that support instructional decisions. For example, grades on a report card can provide an authentic opportunity for the teacher to guide the student into Goal Setting that sets the stage for practicing self-efficacious behavior and decision making.

Goals become motivators and foster positive attitudes toward academic activities when they are specific, clear, and challenging, but attainable through effort. Learning to set and achieve goals is a skill necessary for students to exert control over their academic environment, but students need instruction in setting such goals. When goals are set unrealistically high, even substantial effort produces failure and undermines personal efficacy. Easy goals arouse very little interest or effort. Simple declarations to "do better" or "work harder" do not result in an increase of efficacy or academic progress, no matter how sincere the promise.

Goals that lead to efficacious behavior (see Figure 3.1) must be measurable, firmly anchored in the student's personal values, be achievable without over-reliance on someone else, and contain a time frame for achievement. It is also best for the goals to be published in some form. An unrecorded goal is only a wish and not as likely to be achieved. Effective goals are set in an hierarchal fashion. Long-term goals are needed to provide purpose and directions, but mid- and short-term goals are needed to focus attention and effort. Because time seems to be available in abundance when goals are too far into the future, a series of subgoals, should be arranged in ascending order. The student response in Figure 3.1 clearly illustrates the power of goal setting.

FIGURE 3.1. A STUDENT EXPLAINS THE POWER OF GOAL SETTING

Facilitators: What helped you improve your performance?

> This class helped me to achieve my goals. I didn't even have goals before I came here. It was helpful because I stayed focused and was given help I needed.

There are abundant opportunities to set goals that are authentic: the beginning of a unit; 3 to 5 days before a summative test; at interim; at the beginning of a marking period; at the beginning of a culminating project or activity. The activities discussed in this chapter teach students to set goals that will motivate and enhance personal efficacy.

The beginning of long-term projects is an excellent time for instruction in goal setting. The purpose of the instruction is to teach students a goal-setting routine that breaks difficult goals into smaller related goals. The primary goal is then expressed as a series of intentions that are spread out over time. The instruction in goal setting can be combined with instruction in planning so that students can receive the guided practice and efficacy training they need to achieve their worthy intentions. The goal-setting example in Figure 3.2 combines goal setting with goal visualization.

FIGURE 3.2. A GOAL-SETTING ACTIVITY FOR A LONG-TERM PROJECT

Science Fair Goal Setting

Directions: *Follow the six steps below to identify your science fair goals and to visualize yourself completing what* **you** *intend to accomplish.*

1. In your science journal, write your goal for the science fair project.

   Be positive about what you intend to do and be willing to take a risk.

   Challenge yourself but be realistic—give yourself the opportunity to succeed.

   Break your largest goal into a series of smaller goals—what is your goal for this week? Next week?

2. Break your goal into a series of intentions—what you intend to do between now and the due date to achieve your goal.

   Avoid writing in the negative—don't tell what you will not do.

   Leave out words like "hope," "try," "harder," or "good."

   Be specific about what you intend to do—what will it look like?

3. Set deadlines for each of your intentions and record each step in your assignment notebook.

4. Consider how you might sabotage your own intentions.

   Have you made your goals dependent on you alone?

   How might you cause your own failure?

   What are the chances of you achieving your goals?

5. Relax, close your eyes, and picture yourself completing what you intended to accomplish.

   Notice how you feel.

6. Write a goal affirmation sentence in your journal.

Special education and general education teachers can teach and reinforce goal setting and the hierarchal nature of efficacious goals by requiring students with learning needs to use their Individualized Educational Plan (IEP) goals as part of their goal-setting routine. These students can then periodically reflect on their goal attainment and become an invaluable contributor to the creation of new goals during the IEP revision process. Figure 3.3 illustrates a student who has used his Annual IEP Goal (to establish and maintain an organizational system for school materials) to set his academic goals.

FIGURE 3.3. A STUDENT USES ANNUAL IEP GOALS TO SET ACADEMIC GOALS

Long-Term
End of this school year
(Set at least one goal)

<u>1. I want to get higher
grades but not to high,
maby a C+ or B+</u>

Short-Term
End of third marking period
(Set at least three goals that are concrete,
achievable, measurable, and challenging)

<u>1. Improve my Math Notebook to an A.</u>
<u>2. Raise my hand when I need to speek.</u>
<u>3. Do my hardest homework first, and easiest last,
so I can be done faster, more efficient thus
putting my grades higher.</u>

Why are these goals important to you?
<u>I want to get higher grades, higher my self-esteem;
but I don't want grades to high, my parents would expect more
from me.</u>

What will you do differently to achieve these goals?

<u>Use the straightegie taught in my support classes.</u>

Sometimes, goals are more meaningful if they flow naturally from an honest self-appraisal and have a strong connection to the next stage of a student's life as shown in Figure 3.4.

FIGURE 3.4. A STUDENT SETS GOALS USING ACADEMIC STRENGTHS AND WEAKNESSES

Strengths	Weaknesses
List at least four things you know and do that lead to school success	List at least four things you do or habits you have that get in the way of school success
Study for tests	Compleating all homework
listen to teachers	following directions
hand in all outside projects	ask for help
	paying attention during class

Directions: Set three goals for the fourth marking period. Each goal must be specific, clear, and challenging but attainable through your own efforts. Each goal must be something that is important to you and that you are willing to work toward achieving.

1.
   Must do all homework in eng. math. geo. s.s.

2.
   Study for all tests in Learning to Learn class

3.
   Get no F's or d's on report card

Why are these goals important to you?

   These goals are important to me because I need better grades to pass this year and to go to vo-tech.

What will you need to do differently to achieve your fourth marking period goals?

   I will listen to teachers and make time to study and do home work.

One of the more important functions of goal setting is the connection students begin to make between their school performance and their life aspirations. An example of one student's reflection on her goal attainment is found in Figure 3.5.

FIGURE 3.5. A STUDENT REFLECTS ON THE PURPOSE OF HER GOAL ATTAINMENT

"Goals"

My goals are important to me because I don't want to end up like my older brother, 20 years old and living at home with a slim chance at a real life. I also want to get out of Unionville and into the real world while being able to handle living independantly.

Exercises in goal setting and achievement can be easily related to any subject. The exercises shown in Figure 3.6 are easily adapted to any activity.

FIGURE 3.6. SEVERAL GOAL-SETTING EXERCISES

Expectations

As we read in _____, people have expectations that influence our behaviors. Often the expectations we have for ourselves come from the expectations that others have for us. These expectations influence our behaviors in positive and negative ways.

Directions:

1. Identify three people in your life who hold expectations for you. Using magazines or personal drawings, find a picture or symbol of each person. Be sure to include yourself on the list.
2. Affix the pictures to a page in your Thinking Journal and write an expectations statement that each would have of you.
3. Develop a response statement that each would have if you improved your self-efficacy skills.
4. Write a paragraph in your journal describing your feelings about meeting the expectations of the people in your life.

◆

Thinking Journal Prompts Directions: *Complete the following statements in your Thinking Journal.*

The Math goal I was most focused on this week was _____.

It was hard for me to _____.

I was surprised to learn _____.

The strategy that helped me the most was _____.

◆

Smoke and Mirrors

1. Self Questioning:

   What are some good things that could happen if I improved my Social Studies test scores?

   What are some bad things that could happen if I improved my Social Studies test scores?

2. Set Goals:

   Long-Term (End of School Year) _____

   Mid-Term (End of First Semester) _____

   Short-Term (End of First Marking Period) _____

3. Affirmation—I will share my goals with _____

4. Reflection—I will discuss my progress toward my goals on
   _____ (date)

REFLECTION

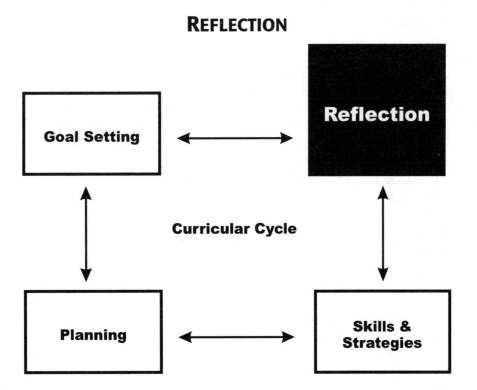

Curricular Cycle

There are various entry points within the recursive pattern of Reflection, Goal Setting, Planning, and metacognitive uses of Strategies. Teachers should decide the best entry points for instruction based on the needs of the student and the demands of the general curriculum. Deciding to begin with Reflection requires teachers to identify opportunities for instruction in Reflection. These opportunities become apparent during liaison meetings, cooperative planning meetings, transition planning, and observations of the students. Curriculum artifacts and teacher knowledge of the general curriculum can provide additional data that support instructional decisions. For example, poor results on an Algebra quiz can prove to be an authentic rationale for the teacher to begin the cycle with Reflection.

Providing time for students to think, talk, and write about their learning, their current level of skill development, their effective use of strategies, and their goal achievement is essential for developing self-efficacy. Learning how to be reflective and to self assess is a necessary precursor and is a fundamental part of personal growth and change. Reflection promotes the union of will and skill and activates a person's willingness to make choices and to accept challenges (Paris, 1994). It allows students to take control of their own progress and learning and to develop the self-efficacy necessary to persist in overcoming obstacles through effort. Through reflection, students can develop:

♦ Self-direction and autonomy

♦ Sense of what they can do and what they can improve

♦ Metacognitive awareness of the strategies they are using

♦ Ability to participate honestly in the evaluation process

Given instruction and the time to reflect on their own performances and accomplishments, students will exercise control over and accept responsibility for the choices they make. Reflective students will develop an internal locus of control, and, because they view their academic progress as their personal obligation, they focus on constructing for meaning and internalizing standards and processes. These students will demonstrate satisfaction with the completion of difficult tasks because they are consciously using their strengths or using bypass strategies to overcome their weaknesses. Reflective students are aware of their levels of motivation, their own skills and talents, and the effort that it takes to persist in the face of difficulties or in the presence of distractions. Reflective students consider and consciously make decisions about their work and study habits. They monitor the effectiveness of the strategies they have chosen and have alternative strategies to choose from if their original choice is not working. Finally, these students are knowledgeable about their successes and failures, plan for future improvement, and map out their intentions. They possess a keen sense of self-efficacy.

Because students can become detached and disengaged if they are not provided frequent opportunities to reflect on their progress and learning, special and general education teachers must model reflective behaviors and provide students with the time to learn and practice the skills involved with reflective thought (see Figure 3.7). Whereas it is important for general education teachers to plan and embed frequent opportunities for reflection in to everyday instruction, it is critical for special education teachers to do so. The school day is filled with opportunities for reflection. Some of these opportunities are:

FIGURE 3.7. A STUDENT REFLECTS ON HIS USE OF STRATEGIES

Am I Where I Want To Be?

Directions: Prepare for a conference with the instructor by thinking about the answers to these questions.

- Are you using your strategies regularly?

  Yes. There are helping me get my work done.

- Are the strategies making a difference in your school success?

  Yes. I am getting better grades.

- Do you still need to strengthen any of the categories?

  Yes. Math. I need a better grade.

- Before and after summative evaluations;
- Before and after formative assessments;
- Before, during, and after projects;
- Before, during, and after reading;
- Before and after parent conferences;
- At the beginning and end of a marking period.

To become reflective thinkers, students need an environment that allows for setbacks and errors. The students must have the vocabulary of reflections and abundant opportunities for validation. Teaching students a simple reflective routine and then using that same routine throughout the school year helps the process of reflective thought become a routine. One such exercise is shown in Figure 3.8.

FIGURE 3.8. A STUDENT REFLECTION ROUTINE

Read your IEP goals and your goal-setting pyramid. Complete a journal entry answering the following questions:

- **Progress:** Have you reached your goals? Why or why not?
- **Facilitator:** What is helping you or what did you do to get closer to or reach your goal?
- **Obstacles:** What is in the way or is slowing you down as you try to reach your goal?
- **Growth:** What did you learn in the past weeks that you can use in the next weeks?
- **Intentions:** What will you do differently in the future?

Progress: I have reached only one of my goals and I think
            I need to rephrase the other two.

Facilitator: I got my assignment book signed; Mrs.
               Eisenberger helped me do that by nagging.

Obstacles: Constant need of organization, & hatred for
            English.

Growth: I need to keep getting my assignment book signed,
         organize my notebook at least once a week.

Intentions: Personally, next year, I will change . . .

A simple and efficient method of reflection is to have students summarize their intentions, formalize those intentions into a list or journal entry, and to periodically reflect on their ability to maintain those intentions. Figure 3.9 is an example of this student-teacher interaction. Teachers can keep students grounded in reality by suggesting reflection in areas the student may not have considered.

**FIGURE 3.9. A STUDENT IDENTIFIES HIS INTENTIONS
AND A TEACHER RESPONDS**

Directions: List three intentions for third marking period and explain how you feel about your chances of being successful in keeping the intentions you identify.

I intend to bring up my grades in Afro and Geometry to a C.
1. I will practice my geometry work.
2. For Afro I will hand work in on time.
3. Geometry I will do my homework more often and when I need help I will ask for it.
I cause my own failure because I dont do my work like I'm suppose to. I feel good about my chances of achieving, if I do what I said I would my grades should come up to a C.

I think you might also take a really hard look at your attendance patterns. People who come to school regularly usually do much better than those who don't.

Mrs. E

One of the best opportunities for reflection follows a summative evaluation. If students are to exercise control over their academic progress, a method of critiquing tests needs to guide students through an examination of their preparation. Even when a students do well on a test, they can profit from a reflection on their performance. Figure 3.10 is one method of student reflection about test performance.

FIGURE 3.10. A STUDENT CRITIQUES HIS TEST PERFORMANCE

1. ANALYSIS (✖)	3. POSSIBLE SOLUTIONS (✍)
✔ I should have started to prepare sooner than I did.	Begin post-it process as soon as Chapter is assignment.
___ I did not schedule enough time for preparation.	Do all of the hard assignments in Learning to Learn
___ I did the teacher-assigned homework and thought my preparation was adequate.	
___ I should have prepared a splashdown.	
___ I should have picked a different strategy for preparation.	
___ I prepared for recognition when I needed recall.	
___ I was overconfident.	
___ I studied the wrong information	
___ I had trouble understanding the questions or instructions.	
✔ I had trouble with the format of the test.	Ask for assistance to clarify the test.
___ I made careless mistakes.	
___ I ran out of time.	
✔ I guessed too much.	
✔ I choked or "blanked out" during the test.	Talk out chapter with study partner and identify key information
✔ I was unfamiliar with parts of the test.	
✔ I remember seeing the material but could not "pull" the information from my memory.	
___ I misinterpreted what some of the questions were asking.	
___ Other _____	

2. CONCLUSIONS (✎)

<u>I need to study all critical information</u>
—<u>I need to ask for clarification.</u>
—<u>I need to start preparing for the tests as soon as we start</u>
   <u>another chapter.</u>

Reflection does not need to be lengthy to be effective and to promote efficacious behavior. Figure 3.11 shows several short reflections.

FIGURE 3.11. PROMPTS FOR REFLECTION

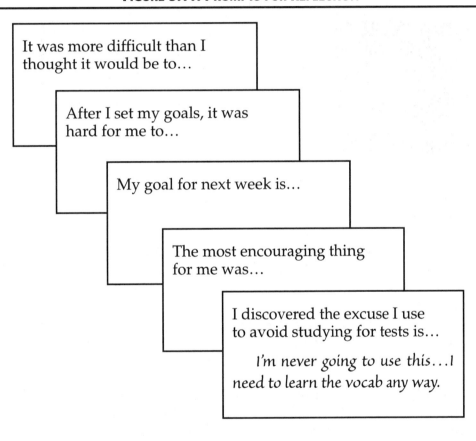

It was more difficult than I thought it would be to…

After I set my goals, it was hard for me to…

My goal for next week is…

The most encouraging thing for me was…

I discovered the excuse I use to avoid studying for tests is…

I'm never going to use this…I need to learn the vocab any way.

PLANNING

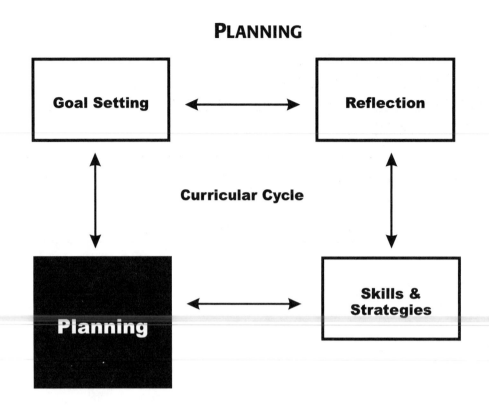

There are various entry points within the recursive pattern of Planning, Goal Setting, metacognitive uses of Strategies, and Reflection. Teachers should decide the best entry points for instruction based on the needs of the student and the demands of the general curriculum. Recognizing where to enter this recursive cycle, and the direction in which to move through the cycle, requires teachers to identify opportunities for instruction. These opportunities become apparent during liaison meetings, cooperative planning meetings, transition planning, and observations of the students. Curriculum artifacts and teacher knowledge of the general curriculum can provide additional data that support instructional decisions. For example, a student's failure to complete and submit homework provides authentic opportunities for the teacher to begin the cycle with Planning.

Planning is the process of combining multiple learning strategies to accomplish academic goals. To plan effectively, students must have a variety of strategies from which to choose and the time to reflect and consider what they would like to achieve. Planning skills include predicting, organizing, and checking. Students who are efficacious planners sequence the actions they will take to meet the demands of a particular task. They select specific strategies that are appropriate for the task or combine several strategies into a workable scheme. They are also able to monitor the effectiveness of their plans and adjust or correct when necessary, dropping and replacing strategies that are not working well. Students who have a strong belief in their efficacy are quicker to discard strategies that are not working, and they consistently and effectively apply what they know (Bandura, 1997).

Because many students with learning needs have difficulty shifting flexibly among different approaches, difficulty coordinating the strategies needed to learn effectively, and difficulty identifying useful planning and checking strategies, specific instructions and guided practice are necessary. In school, authentic opportunities abound to teach students the skills needed to be efficacious planners. One way to teach students planning skills is to have them identify the obstacle they believe is preventing learning and to have them plan a solution. Teachers should help extend the plan into a more complete solution. One student's plan is shown in Figure 3.12.

FIGURE 3.12. A STUDENT IDENTIFIES AN OBSTACLE AND PLANS THE SOLUTION

I want B level grades

Obstacle	Solution
Not on task—Poor listening.	Sit close to the front in all classes or close to the teacher.
	You might also write down what the teachers says. Mrs. E

Students need opportunities to reflect on their planning skills and to identify areas of weakness. Teachers need to teach students to plan just as they would teach any other skill. In Figure 3.13, a student reflects on his skills and identifies an area needing correction.

FIGURE 3.13. A STUDENT MONITORS HIS PLANNING SKILLS

4 = Mastered: I do this automatically. This is part of my school behavior. No one has to remind me.

3 = Good: I know how to do this but I sometimes have to be reminded. Even though I know this will help me be more successful, I don't do this automatically.

2 = Needs Work: I know I should do this but I often need to be reminded. I only do this when an adult suggests this or reminds me it needs to be done.

1 = Not Yet: I only do this when I am forced to or when I am being observed. I refuse to do this or I do not think this is necessary for me.

Comments: Student:
<u>I think I have improved in most areas besides reading directions.</u>

Skill Area	Student	Teacher
Self-Assigned Homework		
Writing	1	1
Projects	1	1
Practice	3	3
Test Preparation	3	3
Keeping Track		
Homework	4	4
Projects	4	4
Test Preparations	3	3
Materials	4	4
Grades	3	3
Strategy Repertoire		
Names, Steps	3	3
Variety	3	3
Matches Learning Style	3	3
Monitors Effectiveness	3	3

Because many students with learning needs have difficulty organizing multiple strategies into a coherent plan, a framework may need to be given to the student. Figure 3.14 is an Objective Test-Taking Cycle frame.

FIGURE 3.14. A STUDENT PLANS FOR THE MANY STRATEGIES NEEDED TO PREPARE FOR A TEST

Steps	Possible Strategies			Personal Plan
1. Set Goal: target a grade establish a time frame commit to strategies	(Conferencing)	Journalizing	Pyramid	conference
2. Identify the key information	Graphic Organizer Clustering Math Attack Color Coding	Cued Notes Highlighting Flash Cards Skimming	3-Fold Page Cornell Notes (Post-Its) Muscle Reading	post it's
3. Memorize the information	Walk About Do & Redo Acronyms Oral Rehearsal	Study Partner Peer Teacher Splashdown 3-Fold Page	Overlearning Write/Read (Key Word Pic.)	keyword pic.
4. Check memory	(Practice Test) Oral Retrieval Walk About	Study Partner 3-Fold Page Flash Cards	Cover & Recite Splashdown Computer Drill	practice test
5. Adjust target grade	Reward Yourself	Goal Setting	(Accepting Feedback)	Accepting feedback
6. Repeat Steps 3–5	I will repeat: 1 (2) 3 4 5			2 times
7. Take Test	Visualizations Eliminate Options (Peek-a-boo) Using Margins	Splashdown (Steal It) Triage Easy to Hard	(Oral Retrieval) Cued Notes SCORER Fore/Back	peek-a-boo steal it—talk it
8. Critique Test Performance	Reward Yourself (Skill Evaluation)	Conclusions Requesting Help	5 Whys Consequences	Critique
9. Adjust Strategies	Responding to Persuasion Responding to Help (Decision Making) Requesting Help			
Repeat the cycle				

Students need time to reflect on planning, but the reflection need not be extremely time-consuming. Figure 3.15 shows several quick but thought-provoking prompts for thinking about planning.

**FIGURE 3.15. SEVERAL QUICK PROMPTS
FOR REFLECTING ON PLANNING SKILL**

Before I set up my plan, I wish I had been told more about…

My goal for next week is to plan…

I organized all my materials for math class by…

This week was special for me because I am getting better at planning for…

Three things I want you to notice about my plan are…

☞ _____

_____

☞ _____

_____

☞ _____

_____

I was surprised to learn that planning helped me to…

It was hard for me to learn… to write in my assignment book all the time. To me, the assignment notebook was a waste of time if you have no homework to list.

STRATEGIES

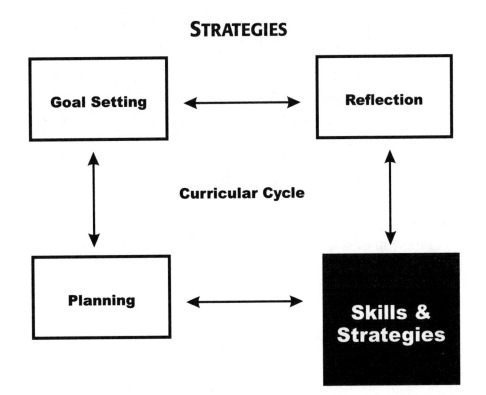

There are various entry points within the recursive pattern of metacognitive uses of Strategies, Goal Setting, Planning, and Reflection. Teachers should decide the best entry points for instruction based on the needs of the student and the demands of the general curriculum. Recognizing where to enter this recursive cycle, and the direction in which to move through the cycle, requires teachers to identify opportunities for instruction. These opportunities become apparent during liaison meetings, cooperative planning meetings, transition planning, and observations of the students. Curriculum artifacts and teacher knowledge of the general curriculum can provide additional data that support instructional decisions. For example, when a student asks a question of his or her support teacher that is better answered by the general education teacher, an authentic opportunity for instruction of a self-advocacy strategy is presented.

Learning strategies are tactics and self-management processes that individuals use while learning. The use of strategies requires effortful processing and is difficult for students unless efficacy skills are in place. Students with learning needs are generally weaker in the number of learning strategies that they know and use spontaneously than their same-age peers who do not have learning needs (Meltzer, 1993). Students with learning needs are less able to select strategies that match academic tasks. These students do not readily make connections between their efficacious use of the strategies and their success in a task (see Figure 3.16), often attributing success to external forces such as an "easy" test. It is critical for general education and special education teachers to teach the student to make the connection between the application of a particular strategy and success in an academic task.

FIGURE 3.16. A STUDENT DESCRIBES THE DIFFICULTY INVOLVED WITH THE ACQUISITION OF A NEW STRATEGY

Getting my assinmnet notebook signed is important to me because Mrs. Eis. said it would help me stay organized, also, part of my Learning to Learn grade relys on it. I will know I achieved it if Mrs. Eis. stops telling me to get it signed and . . . . . . congradulates me for getting it done. It is challenging because I am very lazy.

Students with learning needs are also less able to learn strategies effortlessly. They are clumsy in their execution and application, especially if the strategy is new. Because the initial use of strategies requires an increase in work time, these students will abandon strategies too soon and persist in using less effective strategies. The efficacious use of strategies requires a substantial amount of time and effort, and both the special education teacher and the general education teacher must provide guided practice and a substantial amount of feedback during the cycle of learning described in Figure 3.17

FIGURE 3.17. LEARNING A NEW STRATEGY

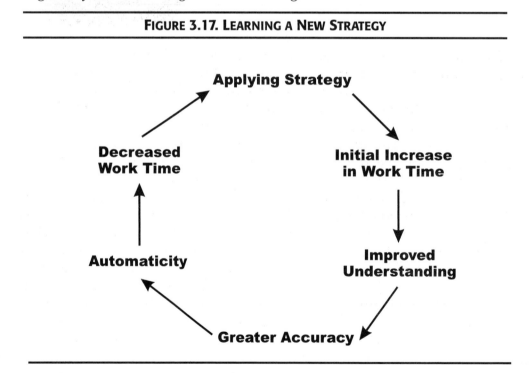

Learning strategies are maintained and transferred to new situations if the students understand their value and can connect the strategy to an improvement in performance (Meltzer, 1992). To produce efficacious students, teachers in special education classes must focus on how to select, use, and monitor strategies, and teachers in general education classes must design lessons that incorporate strategy training and use. The student's reflections can guide needed instruction, as the student's journal entry in Figure 3.18 demonstrates.

FIGURE 3.18. A STUDENT IDENTIFIES A STRATEGY DEFICIENCY AND THE TEACHER RESPONDS

... need to put in effort. I have trouble guessing what will be on a test and when I get nervous I can't think at all. I still need to learn to calm down because I do go into exams prepared.

Good insight. We will pick a "calming" strategy for next marking period.

Mrs. E.

To be most successful when selecting and using strategies, students must be aware of their learning preferences and intelligence strengths. The journal entry in Figure 3.19 demonstrates how choosing strategies based on learning style can benefit students.

FIGURE 3.19. A STUDENT EXPLAINS THE PROCESS OF ADOPTING STRATEGIES BASED ON LEARNING STYLE

I learns better when the material is read out ~~load~~ loud by someone else or myself. My strategies match my learning style. I have a reader for tests when I don't understand a question. I also review for my test outloud before taking it. This gives me clear studying. I also like ~~the~~ to write down my strategy when I used my daily lessons plan. This way I can figure out what I'm doing and how I'm doing it correctly

---

Being aware of how strategies function is another key component in the successful adoption of the processes and skills needed for self-efficacy. One way to ensure that students transfer their strategies with them to other content classes is to have them regularly explain which strategies they find useful. Figure 3.20 is an example of this technique.

**FIGURE 3.20. A STUDENT REVIEWS HIS
STRATEGIES AND EXPLAINS THEIR PURPOSE**

Strategy	*Directions: Circle the strategies you are using and explain how you use each.*

SELF-DETERMINATION:
    Goal Setting/Achievement
    Accepting Feedback
    5 Whys
    (Requesting Help)
    Behavior Checklist
    Responding to Persuasion
    Self-progress Report
    Unhelpful Thoughts
    Positive Self-Talk
	I request help with assignments. I use this to do assignments.

MEMORIZING:
    (Key Word Pictures)
    Highlighting
    (Oral Rehearsal/Retrieval)
    Chunking
    Flash Cards
    Study Partner
    Cover and Recite
    Do and Redo
	Use sounds to help me memorize Use it because I get better grades I use this because it helps me remember

TEST TAKING:
    Test Preparation Routine
    Test Critique
    (Steal It)
    Splashdown
    Eliminating Options
    Test Vocalization
    Math Checklist
	I take stuff off other parts of tests. Helps get better grades

ORGANIZING:
    Assignment & Grade Tracking
    Long-term Assignment Planning
    (Prioritizing)
    Notebook & Locker Organization
    (Hard to Easy)
    Easy First
    Materials Management Checklist
    Post-It Process
    Chunking
	It helps me to get assignments in on time Makes work seem faster I use this on tests and homework

COMPOSING:
  Graphic Organizers
  Steal It
  Oral Rehearsals
  Stop and Think
  Editing Partner
  Power Writing
	I use these to organize and web
	Steal it helps my spelling on test

UNDERSTANDING:
  Post-It Process
  Stop and Think
  Cornell/3-Column Note Taking
  Math Attack
  Muscle and Reciprocal Reading
	In Math Homework I use this.

When students' strategies become automatic, a shift in thinking occurs. The students begin to discuss their use of strategies as part of their abilities. This shift is clearly demonstrated in Figure 3.21.

FIGURE 3.21. A STUDENT DESCRIBES HER SUCCESS AFTER A YEAR OF INTENSIVE STRATEGY INSTRUCTION

What have you learned this year that you will be able to use next year?

> I have learned that I actually **can** do good in school. I think last year I underestimated my abilities and now I am using my abilities to my advantage.

Is your bank of strategies full enough to meet next year's academic demands?

> For now, my strategy bank is full enough but I hope when I hit a problem I will find a new strategy to add to help me out.

To become comfortable with strategies and to make them part of their efficacious patterns, students need to be aware of how they use strategies to learn, organize, and control the environment in which they work, and to transfer those strategies into other areas of their lives. Simple, quick reflections, as shown in Figure 3.22, reveal how well the students are acquiring strategies.

**FIGURE 3.22. STUDENTS EXPLAIN HOW STRATEGIES
ENABLE THEM TO EXERCISE CONTROL AND LEARN**

Three strategies that I used today are…

☞ _____
_____
☞ _____
_____
☞ _____
_____

This week, I wished I had a better strategy for…

I was surprised to learn that…
there are strategies to help me learn things. I learned rules for grammer.

Strategies that work

Chairs and Place
I sit by my self so I can consanetrate

Task

Math class doing math problems—less socializing

Other Uses

Science—my best friend is in that class and I tend to goof more with her.

_____

REFERENCES

Bandura, A. (1997). *Self-Efficacy: The Exercise of Control*. New York: W.H. Freeman.

Beyer, B. K. (1991). *Teaching Thinking Skills: A Handbook for Secondary Teachers*. Fairfax, VA: Allyn and Bacon.

Black, H., & Black, S. (1990). *Book II—Organizing Thinking: Graphic Organizers*. Pacific Grove, CA: Midwest Publications.

Bloom, B. S. (1976). *Human Characteristics and School Learning*. New York: McGraw Hill.

Brooks, J. G., & Brooks, M. G. (1995). *In Search of Understanding: The Case for Constructivist Classrooms*. Alexandria, VA: Association for Supervision and Curriculum Development.

Canady, R.L., & Retig, M. D. (1996). *Teaching in the Block: Strategies for Engaging Active Learners*. Larchmont, NY: Eye On Education.

Choate, J. S. (1997). *Successful Inclusion: Proven Ways to Detect and Correct Special Needs*. Boston: Allyn and Bacon.

Conti-D'Antonio, M., Bertrando, R., & Eisenberger, J. (1998). *Supporting Students with Learning Needs in the Block*. Larchmont, NY: Eye on Education.

Costa, A. L. (1985). *Developing Minds: A Resource Book for Teaching Thinking*. Alexandria, VA: Association for Supervision and Curriculum Development.

Costa, A. L. (1990). *The School as Home for the Mind*. Palatine, IL: Skylight Publishing.

Deschler, D. D., & Schumaker, J. B. (1984). Learning strategies: An instructional alternative for low-achieving adolescents. *Exceptional Children, 52*, 583–590.

Ellis, E. S. (1991). An instrumental model for teaching learning strategies. *Focus on Exceptional Children, 23*, 1–24.

Frank, A. R. (1973). Breaking down the learning tasks: A sequence approach. *Teaching Exceptional Children, 6*, 16–19.

Garavaglia, P. (1993). How to ensure the transfer of training. *Training and Development, 47*, 66.

Gaskins, E., & Elliot, T. (1991). *Implementing Cognitive Strategy Training Across the School*. Philadelphia, PA: Brookline Books.

Geocaris, C. (1996). Increasing student engagement, A mystery solved. *Education Leadership, 54*, 72–75.

Goldstein, A. P., Sparfkin, R. P., Geoshaw, J. N., Klein, P. (1980). *Skill Streaming the Adolescent: A Structured Approach to Teaching Prosocial Skills*. Champaign, IL: Research Press Company.

Hughes, C. (1999). Helping adolescents with learning disabilities become strategic learners. *Bridges–Research into Practice.* University Park, PA: Penn State.

McCarney, S. B., Tucci, J. K. (1990). *Study Skills for Students in Our Schools.* Columbia, MO: Hawthorn Press.

Meltzer, L. (1992). *Strategy Use in Students with Learning Disabilities: The Challenge of Assessment, Strategy Assessment and Instruction for Students with Learning Disabilities: From Theory to Practice.* Austin, TX: Pro-Ed.

Meltzer, L. J. (Ed.). (1993). *Strategy Assessment and Instruction for Students with Learning Disabilities—From Theory to Practice.* Austin, TX: Pro-Ed.

Miles, D. D., & Forcht, J. P. (1995). Mathematical strategies for secondary students with learning disabilities or mathematics deficiencies: A cognitive approach. *Intervention in School and Clinic, 31,* 91–96.

Paris, S., & Ayers, L. R. (1994). *Becoming Reflective Students and Teachers with Portfolios and Authentic Assessment.* Washington, DC: American Psychological Association.

Polloway, E. (1996). Treatment acceptability: Determining appropriate intervention within inclusive classrooms. *Intervention in School and Clinic, 31,* 133–144.

Roy, P. A. (1990). *Students Learning Together.* Richfield, MN: Patricia Roy.

4

Assessing Student Growth in the General Curriculum

The mandates of No Child Left behind (NCLB) require adequate yearly progress. This significantly changes both the role of teachers and the purpose of assessment. Assessment should no longer be seen as only a summation of what content the student has learned; but in addition, formative assessment must provide accurate and useful diagnostic information to both students and their teachers about what has been learned. Assessment can no longer be used solely as grading for the purpose of advancement. Assessment data must be rich enough and specific enough to allow students and their teachers to accurately track growth over time and to plan a program of improvement during subsequent lessons and assignments. Assignments must now be clearly linked to content standards and, when completed, provide information about what students know, understand, and are able to do. Assessments must be broadened to include monitoring the degree to which students use a skill and finding out if students are applying the knowledge and skills they have been taught. Assessment is still important for summing up all the skills and concepts students have learned over a particular period. It must also be a process of gathering evidence about learning and growth; it should be used to provide students with the unambiguous feedback they need to assess their own learning then plan for and make improvements. Assessment, in this expanded format, provides students, teachers, and parents with information about what students currently know, understand, and are able to do in the context of a particular area of study.

Both NCLB and Individuals with Disabilities Education Improvement Act (IDEA '04) compel educators to focus on two current initiatives. The first is the need to optimize learning for all students by providing standards-driven, differentiated instruction. The students must know the standards and their current levels of proficiency within the standards. Although not all children will be able to attain the state-mandated standards, all students should be working toward the same standards. The second initiative compels educators to make available and use accurate, useful, unambiguous data about learning to design and differentiate assignments and assessment tasks. These tasks must provide multiple opportunities for students to learn. The data these assignments and assessments provide must be communicated to students, their teachers, and their parents so reflection and progress can occur.

NCLB has its flaws, and conflict exists between the mandates of NCLB and IDEA '04. However certain realities are with us:

♦ Educating all children, including those with serious learning and behavior difficulties has become everyone's job. Both national and state governments expect that, to the fullest extent appropriate, disabled children will be educated with their nondisabled peers.

♦ Students with learning needs of all types and degrees are now being educated in general education classrooms, and inclusion has become and will continue to be an integral part of public education.

♦ Children will not be excluded from standardized state testing unless the nature or severity of the handicap is such that, even with supplementary aids and services, measurable academic progress has not occurred.

♦ Schools will be required demonstrate annual progress, and students with identified learning needs will be required to demonstrate meaningful yearly progress toward the achievement of the standards as defined in their individualized educational plans.

Under both NCLB and IDEA '04, curriculum based on state standards concerns itself with content outcomes (what students know, understand, and are able to do) and performance accountability (the extent or degree of mastery). Both legal mandates force educators to ensure access for all students to an appropriate education and prepare all students to take the test. Educators must examine their practices and expand their own assessment skills so that they can teach their students how to diagnose and overcome problem areas, persist by maintaining effort, choose the most effective and efficient preparation techniques, and persist in the face of frustration or failure. Teachers must develop their own diagnostic and formative assessment skills so they can differentiate their instruction, provide appropriate interventions and accommodations, as well as set high—but appropriate—expectations for success.

Curricula, even standardized curricula, have a degree of tolerance. The tolerance, a narrow band of what is perceived as normal or average learning by a teacher, varies and depends on a teacher's training, ability to differentiate instruction, and willingness to adapt to the learning needs of the students. Lowering standards and expectations of success serves no one and is not the purpose of developing differentiated lessons, assignments, and assessments for students. Classroom interventions and differentiated instruction level the playing field and allow all students to interact with the curriculum at the highest levels possible for that student. The rationale for writing accommodations to a curriculum is, in fact, to allow students to have a greater likelihood of achieving success by providing bridges to rigorous content standards without lowering expectations.

Unfortunately, many people enter into the debate over the fair use of accommodations without being completely aware of what accommodations are intended to be. When accommodations are appropriately designed and effectively used, they level the playing fields for students who have learning differences or disabilities, but they do not change or excuse students from meeting curriculum-content standards. They fulfill one or more of the following functions:

♦ Assist the student to compensate for the intellectual, physical, sensory, or behavioral challenges.

♦ Allow access to all aspects of the school program.

♦ Allow the student to use current skills while promoting the acquisition of new ones.

♦ Prevent a mismatch between the student's skills and the general education lesson content.

♦ Reduce the level of abstraction to make content relevant to the student's current and future life.

Accommodations are changes in standard operating procedures, are hierarchical in nature, and follow naturally from the student's learning difficulties. The accommodations should be in place for instruction, but are often critical during assessment. Without the accommodations, it is most likely that assessments will reflect the disability or the handicap instead of the degree to which the student knows, understands, or is able demonstrate the content standards.

Although a few students will require specific accommodations for assessment and some instructional modifications, all students would benefit from differentiated lessons. One way to design differentiated instruction is to use formative assessment in conjunction with the curriculum ladder in Figure 4.1.

Figure 4.1. Curriculum Ladder for Planning Differentiated Instruction*

Individual Teachers examine data and make instructional design decisions	*Differentiation*	*Example*
1. Has the student mastered the content? Is the student working at an expanded abstract level?	Enrichment assignment/ activities provided	Student chooses an aspect of the content that is interesting and contracts to do in depth research on that topic
2. If not, has the student mastered pieces of the unit of instruction? Will there be times during the unit when the work will be too easy for this student?	Flexible grouping is provided during a Differentiated Thematic Unit.	Student is given advanced levels of problems to be solved during guided practice.
3. If not, does the student have the prerequisite skills in place to make grade appropriate progress? Are the student's skills sufficient to meet the demands of this unit?	No differentiation needed.	Student receives the whole curriculum as it has traditionally been delivered.
4. If not, can the student make appropriate instructional progress with interventions or remediation?	Intervention/ remediation in place.	Student is given small group instruction in how to take notes from a text.

5. If not, can the student do the same activity and achieve the same standard but with different materials?	Materials adapted	Student is given a copy of stem notes for the material to be memorized.
6. If not, can the student do the same activity and meet the same standards but with differentiated expectations and differentiated materials?	Content instruction differentiated and materials adapted.	Student uses teacher prepared notes, graphic organizers to match information correctly on tests.
School-Based Teams **examine the data and make Decisions**	**Modifications**	**Example**
7. If not, can the student do a similar activity? Student is working toward mixed standards— 80% modified.	Objective changed (fewer or different) with short bridges to the curriculum.	Student orally reports 10 facts.
8. If not, can the student do a similar activity but with adapted materials? Student is working toward the standard.	Objective changed & materials changed with short bridges to the curriculum— IEP goals in place.	Student produces a visual of a historic event to share with the class.
9. If not, can the student do a different, parallel activity or product?	IEP goals.	Student participates in a group research project as the materials organizer.
10. If not, can the student do a different activity in a different section of room?	IEP goals with setting adaptation.	Student uses a computer game matching words to pictures.
11. If not, can the student do a functional activity in a different section of the school?	IEP goals with location adaptation.	Student delivers attendance bulletin to classroom teach-ers.
12. If not, can the student be educated in the mainstream?	Location changed.	Student is educated in a separate facility.
*Adapted from BeBoer-Haller, Project Dakota Outreach, Tailor Made Intervention Training and Consultation Services.		

Critics of special education may be correct when they blame special educators for lowering standards of instruction. It should be a relatively rare occurrence when curriculum goals and objectives are modified for students. Only when multidisciplinary teams decide that students are unable to learn the critical skills and concepts of content standards should modifications be made. Unfortunately, team members can be more concerned with making school more pleasant and easy for the student rather than maintaining appropriately rigorous content supported by scaffolded instruction, or the specially designed instruction of the IEP. Using the Curriculum Ladder can help decision-makers use concrete criteria when deciding to differentiate rather than modify curriculum. Using defensible criteria for modifying curricula can help educators avoid minimizing a student's program or making the course of study so simple that it is without opportunities for the students to engage in appropriate struggle, a condition that is necessary to the development of self-efficacy.

When students with learning needs are discussed, the topics of fair assessment and grading are never far behind. The question most often posed is, "Is it fair to grade students the same way if differentiated assignments and assessment have been given?" The answer is simple. Not only is it fair, it is the only legal option teachers have. If the differentiated lessons are sound—that is, if the lessons are based on documented need and supported by assessment evidence that differentiated activities and assignments yield growth in the standards—then students' grades will represent growth over time. All students should take tests and quizzes and engage in performance tasks to demonstrate what they know, understand, and are able to do. Some teachers handle the fairness question by adapting individual grading criteria and assigning separate grades for process and product. For the most part, teachers who accept the diversity of their students, with or without special needs, are more likely to provide *all* students with the strategies needed for learning and varied opportunities to accurately demonstrate what has been learned.

Some teachers feel compelled to report, in some way, that the course of study they deliver has been differentiated and no longer represents what they consider typical learning. These teachers want clarifying statements included that somehow convey that the student with learning needs really didn't work as hard as the other students. Legally, the only time a district *can* consider putting such a clarifying statement on a report card is if the course has been modified for the student. Differentiated instruction and simple accommodations need not be described on the report card. They will have been described on the IEP or in the 504 Service Agreement. It is actually discriminatory to designate on a transcript that a student has learning needs or that the curriculum had been modified in some way for the student. The focus of assessment is to measure growth over time and to communicate that growth to the student, his parents, and other teachers.

Because NCLB, IDEA '04, and good teaching all require continuous progress, educators must develop multiple ways of assessing growth within the curricula with emphasis on formative assessment. The link between the state standards and the local curriculum must be made explicit so that each assignment and activity is an assessment in itself (Elliot, 2000). These curriculum-based assessments (CBAs) should be specific to the objectives from the curriculum itself. They are teacher-constructed, criterion-referenced instruments designed to reflect progress within the curriculum. The data collected by CBAs provide a picture of the degree to which a student has learned the concepts and skills in the curricula and allow an analysis of student performance within a much broader range of normal (Tucker, 1985).

Curriculum-based assessments are also extremely useful for analyzing progress within the general education curriculum. CBAs are diagnostic teaching tools that place emphasis on how students learn and the strategies they use rather than only the final, content product of traditional summative evaluations (Conti-D'Antonio et al., 1998). Most teachers traditionally have used CBAs when determining the starting point for instruction. In heterogeneous classes, at any point in the instructional process, some students may need guided practice, some may need to accelerate, and some may need additional, direct instruction. CBAs have been used by teachers to determine who those learners are and when it's necessary to adjust instruction.

Students need accurate, unambiguous feedback about their academic status to begin the process of reflection. The reflection process can only begin when the student has data to assess his or her status in a class and uses that data to set academic goals. Curriculum-based assessments are powerful learning tools for students to use to increase their knowledge and skills and/or to grapple with the obstacles they experience as they attempt to apply new knowledge and skills. Meaningful summative and formative assessment is one of the keys to student success in a school where the continuous academic progress of all students is a priority. Soundly applied assessment techniques provide an impetus for students to improve their performance. They also provide opportunities to discuss success, failure, and growth toward the self-efficacy students need if they are to make annual progress. Evaluation is the process of reflecting on all the data collected and judging growth in comparison to curriculum expectations or expected standards. Decisions about what assessment methods are used, when they are used, and for what purpose they are used are critical to planning instructional sequences and instructional decisions. Using curriculum-based assessments to guide instruction provides an opportunity to use the Curricular Cycle—Learning to Learn (Figure 4.2) by providing students with information about their current knowledge and skill base, and by directing students to chart and reflect on their progress as well as to work through the cycle toward more self-efficacious action. Assessments yield information that can make schools inclusionary places where growth is possible for all students. Assessments provide information that allows schools to determine which children are outside the perceived band of normal and allow teachers to identify which students needs more practice and which needs enrichment in any given area at any given time.

Figure 4.2. The Curricular Cycle—Learning to Learn

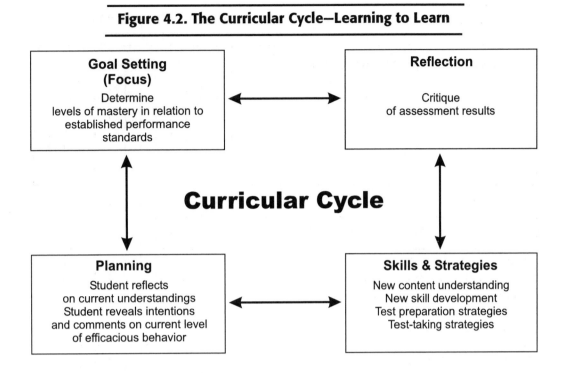

The strategies that have been used successfully with special-needs students can be used to enhance learning for all students. For example, diagnostic teaching, a special education practice, is now shared with general education and frequently called ongoing formative assessment or progress monitoring.

Because progress within the curriculum is basic to both NCLB and IDEA '04, CBAs provide the basis for making instructional decisions by identifying the gaps that occur between what the student is learning and the curriculum-standard and learning goals to be met. They tell educators the rate at which students are learning. CBAs do not necessarily yield scores and are not necessarily used to collapse into student performance grades; but they do provide rich information about the progress students are making within the curriculum. One such CBA, shown in Figure 4.3, was designed by a ninth-grade science teacher as a checkup on behavior during small group activity.

Figure 4.3. A Curriculum-Based Assessment for Checking Up

Skill Behaviors for Group Activities	Student Names
1. Starts to work quickly	
2. Talks in an appropriate tone	
3. Stays on task	
4. Participates without prompting	
5. Shares ideas and materials	
6. Takes turns talking	
7. Criticizes or corrects without personal attacks	
8. Defends ideas without personal attacks	
Developed by Rob Conti-D'Antonio and Joanne Eisenberger	

The rationale for using CBAs to assess progress within general education curriculum is very powerful:

 ◆ CBAs are relevant because students are tested on what is taught.

 ◆ CBAs are less limited than standardized testing. Standardized tests are often out of sync with school curricula. The norming pool is restricted and therefore has a limited use for helping teachers meet the daily instructional needs of all students.

 ◆ CBAs address inclusion mandates. Educators address different developmental rates of learning in one class. Teachers determine if gaps are the result of lack of instruction.

 ◆ CBAs allow for immediate intervention. Teachers determine curricular interventions quickly.

 ◆ CBAs measure more discrete skills that may not be obvious or be able to be disaggregated from standardized assessments.

 ◆ CBAs provide teachers and students with vehicles for reflection. Teachers and students reflect and share in the assessment process.

The potential for frustration and boredom exists in every teacher's classroom. Some students work hard but do not know how to succeed. They do not know how to diagnose and overcome the problems they are having. Other students give up easily and cannot maintain consistent effort. The decisions made to determine the sequences with which to begin instruction, when to reinstruct and provide additional guided practice and remediation, and when to provide enrichment are the most critical yet challenging decisions teachers make. Choosing where to begin instruction is the first step in providing instruction to a broader range of students. Curriculum-based assessments can assist the teacher and provide the data necessary to set up appropriate instructional sequences. This type of formative assessment has been referred to as "providing a window of learning" (Tucker, 1985) for kid watching. Students benefit best from instruction that is at their independent level of learning, but still requires a degree of rigor and appropriate challenge. One of the goals of curriculum-based assessments is to provide learning tasks that support optimum growth. Curriculum-based assessments are tools for *dip sticking*. Dip sticking moments are those during instruction when teachers purposefully check for what students know, understand, and are able to do (Conti-D'Antonio et al., 1998). Differentiating instruction, based on these moments of formative assessment, is critical to offset either frustration or boredom and to provide the education experiences that support rigorous learning and growth toward self-efficacy.

During the development of a CBA, the teacher must focus on the most critical skills and content of the curricula. During CBA construction, the teacher re-examines the major objectives in the curriculum. Typically the steps to developing and using curriculum-based assessments to guide instruction follow this plan:[1]

- Test fluency (both speed and accuracy).
- Record results and have all students chart their outcomes. Performance criteria could be established to determine levels of mastery. In other words, decide what excellent, good, and emerging work will look like and show it to the students and their parents.
- Select sample critical items from curricula or write some to match the curricula, making sure both *content and process* are included.
- Order the skill/content by difficulty. Write an objective for each.
- Prepare and assign student work that tests the achievement of the objectives. Have students chart their performance, reflect on their growth including their level of persistence, and plan for the remediation of any weak areas by consistently asking the following questions:

---

1 Adapted from *Blankenship, C. (1985).* Using Curriculum Based Assessment Data to Make Instructional Decisions.

- Which students have now mastered the objective and are ready for enrichment or a new topic?
- Which students possess sufficient prerequisite skill to begin or continue working on the objective?
- Which students have acquired the topic but require more practice to achieve mastery?
- Which students lack mastery of prerequisite skill and will need intervention or remediation to benefit from instruction on the objective?

Because process is just as important as content, the real challenge when creating curriculum-based assessments is to assess the process along with the content of the subject. When both process and content at attended to, students are more likely to achieve metacognitive control over their learning. It is especially critical that teachers track and teach their students how to persist in the face of frustration or failure and to attend, specifically to test preparation and test-taking strategy skill acquisition. See Appendix I for strategies for reflections, goal setting, test taking, and test preparation. Appendix II includes suggestions for curriculum-based assessment formats.

This is what the following social studies list looks like when the teacher attended to both skills and processes:

- Name and describe the memorization strategies you use to recall the facts of this unit.
- Compare an event from the past with one from the present and explain the similarities.
- Write a topic sentence with supporting details, and a conclusion statement.
- Identify key points in a text about a specific topic.
- Categorize information for presentation.
- Orally compose the summary.

To employ curriculum-based assessments means to use material being taught as a basis for assessing the degree to which it has been learned (Tucker, 1985). Curriculum-based assessments can provide sophisticated yet practical data that can be used during the process for identifying students in need of remediation and enrichment. Curriculum-based assessment can also be used to measure success within the educational system, specifically by analyzing the students' progress in the standards-based curriculum of a local school whose outcomes are known and measurable. They can identify those students who have not internalized test-preparation and test-taking strategies or those who are experiencing difficulty maintaining the effort needed to employ the strategies. When both process and content are assessed, CBAs will tell the teacher and the student which strategies and subject specific test language needs to be learned as well as what learning goals need to be established.

Rates of acquisition and retention of new learning are determined based on progress in the general education curriculum. The point at which the student learns comfortably is of primary importance. The data collected should be aimed at information related to supporting the child to be involved in and progress through the general curriculum.

Example: Curricular goal: Student will increase reading fluency.

- 1.1 grade-level text was used; student read 45 words/minute with 4 errors.

- After 10 weeks of instruction the following data are collected: 52 words/minute with 3 errors (2 words/minute correct/week with 4 errors).

- Retention was also poor in that the student maintained the same level of comprehension.

Another way to examine a student's progress within the general curriculum is by looking at the time it takes to learn. Academic Learning Time, as the formula in Figure 4.4 shows, is the amount of time a student spends in relevant content that he or she can perform at a high level of success (Borg, 1980).

Figure 4.4. Formula for Determining Academic Learning Time

Time on task	The percent of time the student is actually engaged in the task-related behavior.
Task completion	The number of items attempted, whether right or wrong, are counted. The number of attempts is divided by the number required by the task.
Task comprehension	Each task item understood is counted by directly questioning the student. The number of correct answers is divided by total questions asked.
Academic Learning Time	Add the three numbers from the calculations above.
(Thompson, Gickling, & Havertape, 1983)	

Some teachers may be more familiar with analyzing student performance in terms of levels of performance rather than in terms of academic learning time. Individual Reading Inventories or Individual Math Inventories are examples of assessment devices that can provide the teacher with levels of performance within the general curriculum. The following examples are scales for curriculum-based assessments:

Reading Levels	Math Levels
Independent reading 93%–97% accuracy	Independent application & problem solving 85%–100% accuracy
Instructional drill should be 70%–85% accuracy	Instructional drill should be 70%–85% accuracy
Frustration < 70% accuracy	Frustration <70%

Instructional tasks presented in CBAs are selected in terms of the type of task, the number of items in the task, the ratio of known to unknown that translate to performance levels, and the student's performance of the task. General guidelines are followed when using curriculum-based assessments. The process need not be a cumbersome one. The following common-sense procedures can help:

It's helpful to record student behavior in different settings. For example, teachers should consider gathering assessment data in two or more of the following settings:

whole-group instruction	small cooperative groups
labs	centers
individual work	remedial
enrichment	tutorial

Start slowly. For example:

Focus on one skill.   Focus on one or two children.

Focus during independent work time.

Focus on small group rather than whole class.

A variety of CBAs can be developed focusing on a variety of specific skills in different content contexts. Consider the following contexts:

composing	attention
memorizing	questioning
researching	spontaneous language generation
on/off taskness	reading for main idea
working with precision	fluency (speed + accuracy)
metacognition	self-advocacy
constructing for meaning	self-efficacy

Consider the ways in which the student best learns. Some examples follow:

oral rehearsal	peer tutoring
goal setting	high structure
concrete manipulation	

At all levels, well-constructed rubrics, content, and process tests that mimic the language and format of high-stakes tests, portfolios, demonstrations, verbal responses that allow for fuller understanding of the student's thinking process, and checklists can form the basis for assessing progress within a standards-based curriculum and can be made into useful curriculum-based assessments. Math and reading scope and sequence guides, if they are valid representations of the instruction that occurs in the general curriculum, also provide starting points for developing curriculum-based assessments. Rubrics clarify performance expectations and provide a shared guide for the teacher and student as they work through the assessment process. Rubrics can also be used as effective curriculum-based assessments.

Good classroom management is essential during kid watching. Teachers need to remain acutely aware of what is happening in all parts of the classroom at all times, intervening promptly with suggestions and nonverbal cues to support student effort and persistence. Teachers need to respond to individuals while keeping the whole group on task. Effective classroom managers exhibit these key teacher behaviors. For more information on management, see Chapter 2.

- Withitness—remaining aware of what is happening in all parts of the classroom
- Overlapping—being able to do more than one thing at a time; providing fast-paced lessons that use signals rather than distracting verbal prompts to sustain momentum
- Differentiating instruction; providing instruction focused at the correct level of difficulty (Brophy, 1996).

A seasoned teacher will immediately ask about the strategies that can be used to manage the amount of information that can potentially be collected on students during class time. The 5×7 note card strategy is used by Donna Blakeman, Peer Coach with Unionville Chadds Ford School District, and shared here.

Use masking tape to put cards semipermanently on the insides of a manila folder. The cards should overlap so approximately 10 cards can go on each side of the folder. Tape the cards into the folder along the longer side of the card. Students' names are written on the corners of the cards. As teachers circulate and kid watch, they note critical information—what they want to record about each student—on the respective cards. As the cards fill, the cards are peeled from the folder and go directly into the students' files. The teacher does not have to recopy the information, therefore saving valuable time, yet providing a solid basis for reporting out to parents, teachers, and students themselves about the progress each student has made within the general curriculum.

In summary, when using curriculum-based assessments:

+ Focus on what students *can* do.

+ Emphasize what students *learned*, not what was taught.

+ Broaden the range of what is considered normal. (Students progress through developmental stages not discrete, easily measured points in time.)

+ Consider descriptors that can be used consistently when assessing how students are managing new material: *not yet, with guidance, beginning to,* and *independently.*

Figure 4.5 is an example of a curriculum-based assessment used by a teacher to guide instruction. Additional reproducible CBAs can be found in Appendix—Forms. It is important to remember that students do not always make the growth that is anticipated. Even with differentiated instruction, Accommodation Plans and IEPs in place, students fail. This disappointment is the perfect opportunity for reflection and an analysis of the obstacles and facilitators of a student's progress. When self-efficacy and independence are a part of a learner's program, poor school performance can provide the context for goal setting and growth.

Figure 4.5. A Curriculum-Based Assessment Based on Bloom's Taxonomy

Date 12/6/99 Grade 11 Subject U.S. Culture Teacher C-D

Through 1213/99—end of unit evaluation

(Figure continues on next page.)

Indicator	Always (5)	Usually (4)	Sometimes (3)	Occasionally (2)	Noy Yet (1)	Not Applicable (0)	Comments, Observations, Evidence
Perseverence	5	4	③	2	1	0	cuing regularly—not independent
Decreased Impulsivity	5	④	3	2	1	0	good questions
Flexibility	⑤	4	3	2	1	0	listening to each other
Metacognition	5	4	3	②	1	0	annoyed when they had to start
Careful review	5	4	③	2	1	0	most spent time polishing and considering carefully
Problem posing	5	4	③	2	1	0	
Past knowledge	5	④	3	2	1	0	pulled in knowledge from first unit, seemed to be linking knowledge
Enjoyment of Problem Solving	5	④	3	2	1	0	
Precise language	5	4	3	②	1	0	still too much slang

include in grade next to unit

Characteristic	Description	Behavior	Cues/Prompts
Perserverance	Working until solution is reached	Tries again, debates strategy, changes strategies.	Look at this again. What else might you try?
Decreased impulsivity	Pausing to reflect or clarify, requesting more information.	Asks for facts, pauses before answering.	Speed doesn't count. Gather your thoughts. Take your time.
Flexibility	Considering the other points of view, trying new approaches.	Paraphrases others, accepts suggestions or directions, evaluates responses.	Can anyone think of another way to…. Let's try loooking at this another way.
Metacognition	Analyzing, describing one's own thought processes.	Retraces steps, describes strategies and processes used.	Go through the steps aloud. How did you do that?
Careful reivew	Proofing work, comparing work to criteria or exemplar.	Reflects on accuracy of work, checks to ensure accuracy.	Did you compare your work to the rubric? Have you used a peer editor?
Problem posing	Asking quesitons and finding problems to solve.	Wonders. Asks for proof or evidence.	How do you know? What would happen if…?
Past knowledge	Using prior knowledge or past learning.	Makes connection to past experience, content, or ideas	Does this remind you of anything else? Where else might this be useful?
Enjoyment of problem solving	Solving problems with increasing joy and independence.	Positive comments. On task for extended period of time.	You're doing great. Keep working. I'm pleased to see you're hanging in there.
Precise language	Using appropriate descriptive words and labels	Uses analogies, complete sentences, is concise.	**Stop and think**[2] first. What is the scietific work for that?

strategy for next unit
see Joanna E for more

2 For additional information on the Stop and Think process, see Appendix—Strategies.

References

Bertrando, R., Conti-D'Antonio, M., & Eisenberger, J. (1992). *Unionville High School Thinking Skills Project: Final Report.* Kennett Square, PA.

Blankenship, C. (1985). Using curriculum based assessment data to make instructional decisions. *Exceptional Children, 52,* 233–238.

Borg, W. R. (1980). Time and school learning. *Time to Learn.* California Commission for Teacher Preparation and Licensing.   U.S. Department of Education. Washington D.C.

Brophy, J. (1996). *Teaching problem students.* New York, NY: Guilford Press.

Conti-D'Antonio, M., Eisenberger, J., & Bertrando, R. (1998). *Supporting students with learning needs in the block.* Larchmont, New York: Eye On Education.

Earl, L. M. (2001). *Assessment as learning.* Thousand Oaks: Corwin Press, Inc.

Elliot, L. L., & Thurlow, M. (2000). *Improving test performance of students with disabilities.* Thousands Oaks: Corwin Press, Inc.

Ellis, A. (2001). *Teaching, learning and assessment together.* Larchmont, NY: Eye On Education

Gickling, E., & Thompson, V. (1985). Personal view of curriculum based assessment. *Exceptional Children, 52*(3), 205–218.

Gusky, T. R., & Bailey, J. M. (2002). *Developing grading and reporting systems for student learning.* Thousand Oaks: Corwin Press, Inc.

Hill, B., Ruptic, C., & Norwick, L. (1998). *Classroom based assessment.* Norwood, MA: Christopher Gorden.

Salend, S. J., (1995). Treatment acceptability: Determining appropriate interventions within inclusive classrooms. *Intervention in School and Clinic, 31,* 84–90.

Sammons, R. B., & Davey, B. (1994). Textbook awareness and performance profile. *Journal of Reading,* Dec. 1993/Jan. 1994.

Smith, J. K., Smith, L. F., & Lisi, R. (2001). *Natural classroom assessment.* Thousand Oaks, CA: Corwin Press, Inc.

Thompson, V. P., Gickling, E. E., & Havertape, J. F. (1983). The effects of medication and curriculum on task-related behaviors of attention deficit disordered and low achieving peers. *Monographs in behavior disorders: Severe behavior disorders of children and*

youth. CCBD, Series #6, Arizona State University.

Tucker, J. (1985). Curriculum based assessment: An introduction. *Exceptional Children., 52*(3), 199–204.

Wiggins, G. (1998) *Educative assessment.* San Francisco, CA: Jossey Bass, Inc.

5

Helping Parents to Foster Self-Efficacy in their Children

Parents rarely have a window into how teachers and administrators problem solve the demands placed on education by federal legislation such as No Child Left Behind (NCLB), even though those decisions have a direct effect on the success or failure of school as it relates to their children. All schools have in them a wide variety of well-meaning professionals who speak earnestly about *helping* students. However, systems and people who support efficacious behavior are not always seen as champions of the student. "Well meaning adults stack the emotional deck for themselves, often unconsciously, by establishing roles in their school relationships that assure they will get the psychic strokes they need" (Landfried, 1989). People who embrace self-efficacy must acknowledge that their philosophy about independence may not be shared by all the people making decisions about the student. Educators who are committed to teaching students how to be independent and successful must enlist parent support in this process. Parents need to understand how their language and practice impact the efficacy of their children.

A review of the research on parental involvement in education clearly shows that parent involvement in children's learning is positively related to achievement. Additionally, the literature demonstrates that the more intensively parents are involved in their children's learning, the more beneficial are the achievement effects. This is true for all types of parent involvement in children's learning and for all types and ages of students. The goal for parent involvement is to make good decisions about what is best for the student. This can result in land mines involving highly charged, intense discussions involving parents or guardians who can be emotionally strained. Parents may need to be reminded that "the setbacks children endure serve a beneficial purpose in teaching that success usually requires sustained effort" (Bandura, 1997). When working with parents or requesting their support, it's important to clarify goals and to use language that all participants understand. There can be philosophical differences between teachers and parents. For example, both parents and teachers often discuss *helping* the learner. Care must be taken to recognize how much of a detriment one connotation of the word *help* can be, in the long run, to independence. A parent or unenlightened professional can define it as minimizing rigor and standards. Actually, the student must be taught ways to deal with rigor and high standards. Depending on the concerns and problems that surface, some parents may need help to identify the less obvious, but just as challenging, social and emotional issues facing students with learning needs (Lerner, 1971).

The research indicates that to involve parents successfully, schools must offer them a wide range of activities to accommodate different schedules, preferences, and capabilities. Other suggestions for engaging parents include:

♦ Communicate to parents that their involvement and support makes a great deal of difference in their child's achievement, and that they need not be highly educated or have large amounts of free time for their involvement to be beneficial.

♦ Encourage parent involvement from the time children first enter school.

- ◆ Develop parent involvement programs that include a focus on parent involvement in instruction.
- ◆ Provide training and orientation for parents in the strategies their children will need if they are to be successful in school.
- ◆ Make a special effort to engage the involvement of parents of disadvantaged, special needs, and English-language-learning students, as well as other specific student groups.
- ◆ Continue to emphasize that parents are partners with the school and that their participation is needed and valued.

When parental involvement programs were compared, those programs that included an orientation/training component enhanced the effectiveness of parental involvement. Parents were expected to conduct learning activities with their children at home, to assist with homework, and to monitor student progress. However, the research also found that the orientation/training programs with extensive parent training did no better than programs that offer basic training and sometimes experienced considerable attrition (Cotton & Wikeland, 2000).

Student attitudes and social behavior are also positively affected by parent involvement. Although the research is not as extensive as the parent involvement/student achievement relationship, all the studies that addressed attitude and behavior found that parent involvement has positive effects on student attitude and behavior. With passage of NCLB and the continued emphasis on meaningful progress for disabled students posited, it is imperative that educators and parents develop within their children the skills, attitudes, and dispositions necessary to be successful, independent learners. These skills, attitudes, and dispositions build the belief that a person has the necessary abilities to produce quality work through sustained effort—self-efficacy.

The role of parents continues to be imperative under IDEA '04. Successful students usually have parent advocates. The key is to keep the advocacy positive so parents remain supportive rather than combative toward the school. This advocacy is particularly strong among parents of students with learning needs. These were the parents who provided the impetus to stimulate research, legislation, and the expansion of special education public law in the late 1960s and 1970s that ultimately led to the reauthorization of IDEA in 1997 (Schmidt, 1976) and again in 2004. Educators, therefore, should not be surprised with the level of involvement parents of students with learning needs continue to display. Because of the value placed on parents as members of the IEP team, special education and general education teachers will need to help parents recognize that the goal of IDEA '04 is to graduate productive, independent citizens to the greatest extent possible.

Educators will need to include parents in problem solving and goal setting so that efficacy training and reinforcement can occur at home as well as at school. Teachers will need to articulate the benefits of efficacious behaviors, provide concrete and accurate information about their children's progress, and be prepared to encounter opposition from parents and administrators as students who are accustomed to an easy ride express complaints. Parents must also be supported as they struggle with the realization that appropriate, but gradually increasing, rigorous and demanding tasks need to be part of their child's education.

The role of parents in developing self-efficacy within their children cannot be overstated. The focus must remain on the student's progress so that setbacks set the stage for self-efficacy development. Although the happiness and self-esteem of the student are important concerns, these attributes must not become the primary focus. Parents may need to be reminded that developing efficacy requires experience in overcoming obstacles through effort. Educators should encourage parents to foster self-efficacy in their children by exhibiting these behaviors:

- Place a value on education
- Set beliefs about scholastic abilities
- Establish regular homework habits
- Set standards of excellence
- Help with schoolwork at home
- Keep track of academic progress
- Support school-related functions
- Assist with school activities
- Reward efforts
- Prepare children for school (Bandura, 1997)

All participants involved in planning for students should be wary of individuals who want to make themselves indispensable to students. If students perceive their success to be impossible without a specific adult intervention, then a student's road to self-efficacy will be detoured by well meaning, though, personally needy adults. Consider what Bandura lists (Figure 5.1) in *Self-Efficacy: The Exercise of Control* (1997) and the effect teachers' beliefs in their efficacy affect their general orientation toward educational processes as well as instructional activities

Figure 5.1. Teachers' Beliefs in their Efficacy

High-Efficacy Beliefs	Low-Efficacy Beliefs
Optimism about their ability to teach and reach a wide population of students	Pessimism about their ability to influence student behavior and enhance student motivation
Confidence that difficult students are reachable and teachable through extra effort and appropriate techniques	Distrust in their ability to manage the classroom Stressed and angered by student misbehavior
Actively enlist family supports	Contact parents only for punitive sanctions
Work to overcome community influences through effective teaching	Use negative sanctions to get students to workMired in classroom problems
Believe efficacy is an accurate prediction of student achievement	Use strict regulation for classroom management and learning
Enjoy their profession and express satisfaction with their job	Take a custodial view of the job and if they had to do it again, would not choose the profession

It is truly a paradigm shift for some people to think about students as potentially efficacious and independent. This shift in thinking requires a certain conscious effort to communicate as clearly as possible, as often as possible, and to all who will listen that standards and rigor are important for all learners, that appropriate strategies can be taught to learners, and that support does not mean enabling. A clearly articulated learning plan that includes a cycle of goal setting, planning, skill, and strategy instruction and reflection is critical. The parent can provide reinforcement at an appropriate entry point into the cycle of learning at the goal-setting stage, planning stage, or reflection stage. (See Chapter 3 for more information on exercises that support efficacious behavior.)

Besides fostering self-efficacy in their children, parents can also be trained to use many of the strategies that lead children to develop the belief that they have the ability to produce quality work through sustained effort. Appendix I contains strategies that can be employed by both teachers and parents to develop self-efficacy within their children. The strategies that best lend themselves to parent training are:

- ♦ I Can
- ♦ Stop and Think
- ♦ Requesting Help or Accommodations

- Accepting Feedback
- Grade Tracking
- Conferencing
- Responding to Persuasion
- Assignment Tracking

Stop and Think, Requesting Help or Accommodations, Accepting Feedback, and Conferencing strategies are all designed to help students recognize their particular learning strengths and needs problems. Stop and Think technique is an essential strategy for impulsive students who tend to work too quickly and for failure-syndrome students who give up too easily. Requesting Help or Accommodations strategy provides students with the basic steps to help them cope with schoolwork or personal problems. This strategy requires students to analyze their particular problem and to decide on a course of action to solve it. Accepting Feedback is a strategy that enhances students' abilities to listen to feedback and use that information to change or maintain behavior. Conferencing strategy provides students with a method for interacting cooperatively with teachers, peers, and parents. This strategy includes all the essential components of self-efficacy.

I Can, Grade Tracking, Responding to Persuasion, and Assignment Tracking are all strategies designed to promote the attribute of persistence within students. Students will not automatically become persistent because they are given challenging assignments. The I Can strategy provides a process for retraining negative self-defeating internal dialogues (I can't) to positive and more helpful (I can) thoughts. It is helpful when working with students who have experienced years of frustration and failure, or who have been urged to try harder without being taught what it means to be persistent. This is one strategy that could be better taught in the home because it is best taught during a time of calm. Grade Tracking teaches students how to track their academic progress so that they can determine which courses need their attention. Responding to Persuasion is a process that teaches students how to listen with an open mind. This strategy, perhaps, has more application at home than at school. Students who are often overwhelmed by large tasks will find the Assignment Tracking strategy helpful. This strategy requires students to break assignments down into small manageable segments, to distinguish between completed work and work that still must be done at home, and to set a schedule for completing the unfinished work.

Teachers who teach for self-efficacy don't enable. During interactions with parents, teachers must be prepared to give concrete examples of what self-efficacious behavior will and will not look like in their classrooms. This means being clear that parents and teachers avoid tasks that are student tasks. For example:

- Teachers will not put words in students' mouths struggling for the correct answer.
- Teachers will not pick up trash left by students.

♦ Teachers will not make flimsy excuses for children to avoid criticism for lack of discipline from supervisors (Landfried, 1989).

Furthermore, neither parents nor teachers should take on responsibilities that are clearly the student's. Remember, it is the job of the teacher and the parent to foster independence and self-efficacy. That means modeling the assumption of appropriate responsibility. Some responsibilities are the learner's alone:

♦ Students will not be allowed to tune out while the teacher does the talking.

♦ Students will not be allowed to forget assignments without penalty.

♦ Students will not be given credit for sloppy work.

♦ Students will not cheat without penalties.

♦ Students will not take tests and receive grades for work that is too easy.

♦ Students will not be allowed to sleep, read newspapers, or carry on irrelevant conversations during class activities (Landfried, 1989).

Parents who accept the notion that persistence and self-efficacy can be fostered, can be trained to use strategies with their children. This training can occur in a variety of ways. In some instances, the training can occur at the suggestion of the teacher at a parent-teacher conference, students can share the strategy with their parents at home, or some parents may ask for suggestions in helping their children succeed. Parents could be helped to foster their child's efficacy and persistence with Art Costa's model from Habits of the Mind so they can reinforce persistent behavior.

♦ Define, refine, clarify, and analyze the problem, including what information is available and what is missing.

♦ Develop and use a strategy, including backup strategies, and illustrate what success will look like.

♦ Identify appropriate resources, including who to go to for assistance.

♦ Collect evidence that the original strategy is or isn't working, including how much time should pass before an alternative strategy should be used (Costa, 2003).

Regardless of how much coaching a parent has received, the teacher is still the professional. The teacher is the single most influential person in the student's educational life; the teacher is the most important factor in determining student achievement (Wong, 1999). It is crucial for the professionals to keep the focus on self-efficacy and what it means for the student. Teachers must apply the following requirements when planning for instruction for all students:

♦ Rigor will occur in incremental stages to match the skills and strategies the student is learning.

♦ Students will learn to embrace challenge and persist through challenging tasks.

♦ Tasks will be rigorous and engaging (Csikszentmihalyi, 1993).

Parents need to see and hear evidence that their children are learning within a system that supports the highest level of student independence. The teacher's responsibility is to assist as the student moves from goal setting, planning, learning skills and strategies, and reflection stages. Students need to know that they will be taught strategies for reflecting on successes as well as failures, strategies for goal setting and planning, and strategies for managing new information and skills. Students can learn how to set high goals and reach them with systematic application of learning strategies.[1] This contrasts with what typically goes on where "teachers spend significant amounts of time helping students complete homework assignments, study for tests, or clarify" (Hughes, 1999). At best, this short-term tutorial serves to make people feel good. It results in little lasting impact on the student except to ensure dependence on tutoring.

Most importantly, parents must be taught that persistence and self-efficacy are composed of a set of learnable behaviors and that assignments are being designed to provide appropriate but rigorous challenge. After all, providing concrete ways for parents to effectively and appropriately influence growth in their children will produce increasingly self-efficacious parents. With parental reinforcement at home, the likelihood that children will develop self-efficacy greatly increase.

References

Bandura, A. (1997). *Self-efficacy: The exercise of control.* New York: W. H. Freeman.

Brophy, J. (1996). *Teaching problem students.* New York: Harper and Row Publishers.

Canter, L., & Canter, M. (1991). *Parents on your side.* Santa Monica, CA: Lee Canter and Associates.

Cotton, K., & Wikeland, R. (2000). Parent involvement in education. *School Improvement Research Series.* Portland, OR: Northwest Regional Laboratory.

Costa, A. L., & Kallick, B. (2000). *Habits of the mind.* Alexandria, VA: Association for Supervision and Curriculum Development.

Csikszentmihalyi, M., Rathunde, K., & Whalen, S. (1991). *Talented teenagers.* New York: Cambridge University Press.

Eisenberger, J., Conti-D'Antonio, M., & Bertrando, R. (2000). *Self-efficacy raising the bar for students with learning needs.* Larchmont, New York: Eye on Education.

---

1 For explanations of specific learning strategies see Appendix—Strategies.

Hughes, C. (1999, Spring). Helping adolescents with learning disabilities become strategic learners. *Bridges: Research into practice.* University Park: Pennsylvania State University, College of Education.

Landfried, S. (1989). "Enabling" undermines responsibility in students. *Educational Leadership, 47,* 79–83.

Lerner, J. (1971). *Children with learning disabilities.* Boston, MA: Houghton Mifflin.

Louck, H., & Waggoner, J. (1998). *Keys to reengaging families in the education of young adolescents.* Westerville, OH: National Middle School Association.

Schmidt, C., & Foster, G. (1976). *Parent and community involvement: Learning disabilities handbook.* Chicago, IL: University Press.

Schunk, D. H. (1991). Self-efficacy and academic motivation. Educational Psychologist, 26, 207–231.

Wong, H. (1999). *Induction: Helping teachers succeed on the first days of school.* HK Wong Publications Newsletter. Mountain View, CA.

APPENDIX I

STRATEGIES

I CAN

The lack of self-efficacy often limits a student's ability to respond creatively to situations and challenges. To be successful in academic tasks, students need to believe in their ability to achieve. The I Can strategy provides a process for re-training negative self-defeating internal dialogues (I can't), to positive and more helpful (I can) thoughts. Students should be taught the dialogue process during a time of calm and then be cued to use the set of questions when the negative thoughts intrude. Students will need some skill training in rephrasing negative thought to positives before using this strategy in a stressful situation.

STEPS

1. Think of an "I can't" statement that you often make and write it down.

2. Below the statement, list as many thoughts and fears as you can associate with it.

3. Ask and answer these questions:
   - What is a different or more helpful way I can think?
   - How does the new helpful thought make me feel?
   - Is it helpful to keep thinking the new thought? Why or why not?

4. Rephrase the original statement into an "I can" statement.

Some students find it useful to associate a physical "trigger" (snap of the fingers, tap on the forehead) with negative thinking. This trigger becomes associated with the negative thoughts and reminds the student to replace the negative thoughts with positive patterns.

THE POCKET PROCESS

The Pocket Process provides the student with a strategy for delaying thoughts that are interfering with attention and concentration on academic activities. Students are taught to put aside thoughts that are important but not relevant to the task at hand. This strategy should be taught when the interfering thoughts are low stress. The student may need to be cued to use the strategy for several trials before it becomes automatic.

STEPS

1. Identify the mentally distracting thought.

   Some examples might be:

   • Worrying about an up coming math test during English class.

   • Mentally replaying an argument.

   • Dreaming about summer vacation.

2. Write or draw the distracting thought on a piece of paper.

3. Fold the paper into a small square, put it in your pocket, and give yourself permission to think about it later.

4. Over time, replace the written thoughts with a mental process (bracketing):

   • Mentally put a fence around the intruding thoughts.

   • Walk through a gate.

   • Close the gate behind you.

CHAIRS IN PLACE

The Chairs in Place strategy provides students with a method for removing themselves from an area of high distraction to an area more appropriate to the task. It is especially useful when the tasks are not intrinsically motivating or when others are engaged in a variety of tasks resulting in increased noise and movement. Students may need to be cued to use this strategy frequently before they are able to use this independently. The associated strategies of Accepting Feedback and Responding to Persuasion may need to proceed this strategy.

STEPS

1. After choosing a task, stop and think about the best place in the room to focus and concentrate on that task.

2. Take your materials to that location and complete the task. (Sometimes it may be necessary to ask permission to move to the new location.)

3. Some optimal places might be:
   - With your back to the rest of the students
   - Near the teacher, parent, or coach
   - Away from doors, windows, and air conditioners (or other noisy places)
   - Near another student who shares your commitment to the task

4. After completing the task, compare the time needed in the new location with the time need in the old location.

THE THREE-FOLD PAGE

The Three-Fold Page (or 3-Fold Page) strategy gives the student a method of reviewing key information that is interactive and repetitive. With each repetition, the student comes closer to meeting the challenges of a summative evaluation and gains self-efficacy. This strategy combines identification of key information, memorization, and practice with retrieval, and requires students to identify the key information. A process for recognizing the key points may need to be mastered before the student can use this strategy independently.

STEPS

1. Fold a piece of notebook paper into three equal parts to form six columns (front and back).

2. Label each column alphabetically from A to F.

(front)			*(back)*		
A	**B**	**C**	**F**	**E**	**D**

3. Write the key words (the answers to test questions) in column A.

4. Fill in the key information (the test questions) in column B.

5. Fold under column A under so that only B and C show. From memory write the answers to the key information column C. Unfold column A and check your work. Do a math problem to determine your level of readiness.

6. Fold under column C and turn the paper to the back. From memory, write the key information about the key words in column D. Look at column B only after writing all the key information you can from memory. Do a math problem to determine your level of readiness.

7. Lay the page so that only the back shows. Write the key words for each item written in column E. Check your work against column A only after answering all the information you can from memory. Do a math problem to determine your level of readiness.

8. Fold under column D so that only column E and F can be seen. From memory, write the key information in column D. Look at column B only after writing all the key information you can from memory. Do a math problem to determine your level of readiness.

9. Identify any key words or information you are having a difficult time remembering, and prepare a separate three-fold page for them.

10. Repeat steps 3 through 8.

THE THREE-FOLD PAGE (BACK)

F	E	D

THE THREE-FOLD PAGE (FRONT)

A	B	C

CORNELL NOTES

The Cornell Method of note taking provides the student with a strategy for constructing for meaning by transacting with the text while recording information that is self-organized and concise. The Cornell Method enables the student to produce a polished set of notes that is both a record of the material assigned and a study and review guide.

STEPS

1. Date the top of the page and identify the subject and unit being studied.

2. Draw a line 3 inches from the left edge of the paper. (The page is divided into one-third and two-third segments.) Label the one-third column RECALL.

3. Write notes in the two-thirds segment of the page. Take brief notes using key words. Skip lines between main ideas. Leave spaces if an idea is missed or questions arise.

4. As soon as possible after class, read through the notes and fill in any blanks. Highlight the key words and ideas.

5. Fill in the recall column with key words, mnemonic devices, diagrams, or questions.

6. Draw a line across the paper one or two inches from the bottom and label this SUMMARY. Write a brief summary of the notes on this page in your own words.

7. Review the notes daily by folding the page so that only the RECALL column is showing. Repeat the review with only the Key Information Column showing.

EXAMPLE

Earth Science—Ocean Facts 10/15/98	
Recall	**Key Information**
P1 – AAA	5 oceans — Pacific, Indian, Atlantic, Antarctic, Arctic
Deepest?	Deepest — Atlantic
Largest?	
Summary	
Five oceans cover the earth. They are the Pacific, the Atlantic,...	

2-COLUMN NOTE TAKER

Name _____ Subject _____ Date _____

Key Term	Use a few high information words to define or explain the key term.
Summary	

STOP AND THINK

The Stop and Think strategy gives the student a metacognitive process to determine whether they understand a text while they are interacting with it. The Stop and Think strategy is an essential part of many other strategies and frameworks such as *Math Assault, Goal Setting, Muscle Reading*, and *The Objective Test-Taking Cycle*. It may need to be taught and mastered before proceeding to the more complex processes. This is an essential strategy for impulsive students who tend to work too quickly and for failure syndrome students who give up too easily. It is critical for students with low self-efficacy.

STEPS

1. Read a predetermined number of pages, study a picture, or math problem.

2. Stop reading or examining and ask:
   - Does this make sense to me?
   - Where have I seen (heard) of this before?
   - How is this like experiences (problems) I have had before in class (in life, seen in movies, etc.)?

3. Read on (examine more) and stop and think about the next section (or problem.)

Note: Students should be instructed in strategies to use if they do not understand the material or cannot relate the passage to their own experiences even though they have stopped and reflected.

MUSCLE READING

Muscle Reading provides a student with a three-phrase technique for extracting knowledge and information from extended passages in textbooks. A variation of *SQRRR*, this system works especially well for social studies and science texts where embedded language and dense information are the norm. At first, the multistep framework may seem awkward and cumbersome, and it does take time to learn and master. The payoff is less time rereading material and a well-constructed test-preparation study guide.

Phase I—Before you read (5 to 15 minutes depending on length of reading assignment)

1. Preview—Flip through the pages of the assigned reading. Notice section headings, read picture captions, and look at bold face words until you get to the end of the assigned reading. If there is a chapter review at the end of the reading, read it first. If a vocabulary list is included read those words and identify any that you already know. This step is a warm-up exercise, activating prior knowledge.

2. Outline—Notice how the reading is organized. Quickly read the section titles and paragraph headings. Decide whether a mind map, Post-Its, Cornell Notes, or a formal outline will be best to use during the reading and set up the note-taking format.

Phase II—Reading (10 to 30 minutes depending on length or difficulty of the assignment)

3. Read—Visualize the material. Read aloud when you feel your mind wandering. Reading aloud is especially good for complicated material. Sit up and avoid reading in bed except for fun.

4. Underline, highlight, write Post-Its or Cornell Notes, or fill in a mind map or outline as you read.

5. Answer—Write the answers to the questions in the section review, or study guides, or that you asked yourself during the prereading phase. Expand your outline, mind map, Post-Its, or Cornell Notes. Write down new questions as they occur to you. Think of yourself as a detective figuring out what will be on the next test.

Phase III—After you read (5 to 10 minutes depending on detail gleaned from the assignment)

6. Recite—Talk to yourself about what you have learned. Explain as much as you can about each key point you have listed.

7. Review—Within 24 hours of reading the material. Look at your notes, fill in anything that you don't understand, recite some of the main points. Check to see what is already in your memory.

8. Review again—Read your notes once a day for about 5 minutes. Recite the more complicated information.

Based on the work of Ellis, D. B. (1991). *Becoming a Master Student*. Rapid City, SD: College Survival.

GRAPHIC ORGANIZERS[1]

Using Graphic Organizers provides the student with structures that organizes large amounts of information or abstract information into a graphic representation. A student can then use the information on the graphic organizer to prepare for tests, write essays, correct understanding, analyze information, draw conclusions, or make connections.

STEPS

1. The student selects an appropriate "blank" from an assortment provided by the instructor or creates a mind map using circles and connected lines.

2. The student gathers information and places the information onto the graphic organizer in appropriate boxes, columns, circles, etc.

3. The graphic organizer can then be used to prepare for tests, write essays, correct understanding, analyze information, draw conclusions, etc.

EXAMPLES

Function	*Graphic Organizers*
Constructing Knowledge	Semantic Maps including Webbs Debate Organizers
Clarifying/Connecting Details	Core Planning Charts Taba Charts Concept Clarifiers
Recognizing Patterns	Action-Reaction Charts Problem-Solving Structures Cause & Effect Diagrams
Elaborating	Multiparagraph Organizers Mind Maps

---

1 Two Excellent sources of Graphic Organizers are Black, H., & Black, S. (1990), *Book I and Book II—Organizing Thinking: Graphic Organizers,* Pacific Grove, CA: Midwest Publications, and Ellis, E. (1999), *Using Graphic Organizers to Make Sense of the Curriculum,* Tuscaloosa, AL: Masterminds.

MATH ASSAULT

A developing sense of self-efficacy can be undermined by course work that is out of alignment with a student's learning style or level of abstract reasoning. The Math Assault strategy gives a student a systematic, concrete process for solving high-level mathematics problems using both auditory and visual modes. This strategy enables an instructor to detect and correct errors in a student's problem-solving process and ends with a "paper memory" that a student can use in solving other abstract problems. Color-coding paper to organize topics or laminating the model sheets for permanent storage and reference is also useful.

STEPS

1. Write a problem on the top of a notebook page or 6" x 8" note card.

2. Verbalize and record the mathematical steps as you solve the problem.

3. Verbalize the steps again as you write the steps in sentence form beside each step.

4. Use the paper or card for reference when solving similar problems and when preparing for tests and quizzes, or as a cued note system during a test.

	Factor completely $x^2 - 8x + 15$ and check using FOIL
1. (x)(x)	1. x times itself is x^2 so I can write that in each parenthesis.
2. (x –)(x –)	2. The plus sign in front of the 15 tells me both signs will be the same. The minus sign in front of the 8x tells me both signs will be negative. I can write that in each parenthesis.
3. (x – 3)(x – 5)	3. What two numerals will multiply to the last numeral and add or subtract to the middle numeral? 1,3,5, and 15 are the multiples. Three and five add to eight and multiply to 15; I can write 3 and 5 in the parenthesis.
4. FOIL	4. Write the FOIL (First, Outside, Inside, Last) mnemonic under my solution.
5. x^2	5. The first two terms in each parenthesis means x times x. That is x^2.
6. –5x	6. The outside terms in each parenthesis are x times –5. That is –5x.
7. –3x	7. The inside terms are –3 times x. That is –3x.
8. +15	8. The last terms are –3 times –5. That is +15.
9. –5x and –3x are –8x	9. The only like terms are the middle two. –5x –3x combine to –8x.
10. x2 – 8x + 15	10. Write the complete expression and compare to the original problem.

REQUESTING HELP OR ACCOMMODATIONS

The Requesting Help process provides a strategy that allows students to seek assistance so they can cope with information, directions, assignments, and personal problems. Students can use the same basic steps to request their accommodations.

STEPS

1. Decide specifically what the problem is (or what accommodation is appropriate to be requested) and form it into a statement. Be sure to consider the following:
   - Who or what is causing the problem?
   - Why is the accommodation needed and appropriate?
   - What is the effect of the problem on the student's learning or on the student's ability to show what the student knows?

2. Decide whether help (accommodation) is necessary to solve the problem or whether the problem can be solved without help (accommodation).
   - A teacher should help students separate power plays and attention-seeking behaviors from requests for solutions. If the student's goal is to engage in a battle, help is inappropriate. Words such as win or lose, right or wrong, and fair should be avoided if possible.

3. (Optional step) Brainstorm to come up with a list of people who might help and pick one.
   - The teacher should encourage all possible helpers so that the student can choose the best one.

4. Rehearse stating the problem (or accommodation) defined in step 1, and practice asking specific questions.

5. If necessary, make an appointment with the helper chosen and ask that person for assistance.

6. Ask for help or an accommodation.

NOTEBOOK ORGANIZATION STRATEGY

The Notebook Organization Strategy provides the student with a routine to become orderly with his or her materials. The goal is to form the habit of routinely cleaning and filing. Students may need the teacher's assistance in deciding what materials need to be filed and what materials can be discarded.

STEPS

1. Establish the purpose for orderliness—help the student understand the relationship between organization of materials and success.

2. Clean locker, book bag, textbooks as follows:
   - Place all pens, pencils, rulers, calculators, erasers, etc., together in the front pocket of the book bag or in a plastic pouch in a three-ring binder.
   - Divide binder into separate sections for each subject, have a separate pocket folder for each subject, or have a separate spiral notebook for each subject.
   - Date all assignments, notes, worksheets, and place them into the separate subject areas at least once a week. Daily filing is recommended.

Note: Students who complete homework and then cannot find the work need to design a separate system of filing completed homework. These students might benefit from having a homework folder that is separate from the subject area work. That folder should have the completed homework in it and should be empty by the end of each school day.

ACCEPTING FEEDBACK

The Accepting Feedback process provides students with a strategy that enhances their ability to listen to feedback—both positive and negative—and to use that information to change or maintain behavior. If the student is unable to "hear" the feedback, an associated strategy such as *Responding to Persuasion* or *Following Instructions* may need to proceed this strategy.

STEPS

1. Listen carefully while you are receiving the feedback. Take notes, nod your head, or say "mm-hmm" so that the person giving the feedback knows you are listening.

2. Ask questions about anything that you don't understand so that the feedback is specific and clear. Do not argue with the feedback or try to defend and explain away the feedback.

3. Accept the positive feedback and acknowledge the compliment or recommendation.

4. Repeat any suggestions on how to change the negative feedback to positive feedback.

5. Decide what you think about the negative feedback by separating your ideas from the other person's ideas and say your ideas aloud.

6. Decide if you can follow the suggestions and let the other person know your decision.

7. Do what has been decided.

ELIMINATING OPTIONS

The Eliminating Options strategy provides the student with a decision-making guide to identify the distractors on a test. Students can find and cross off the distractors, focus on the remaining options, and improve their chances of a correct response. This strategy can also be used with any assigned work that requires choosing among many options and is an essential skill for students who have a tendency to perseverate. All students should be taught *Response Generation,* reading the stem of the multiple-choice question without looking at the options and trying to answer the question before looking at the options, as a companion strategy.

STEPS

1. After using *Response Generation,* read all the options and find the one that best matches your initial response. If your answer is not an option given on the test, use the following guidelines to eliminate the options:

   • Cross off the answers that are obviously wrong.

   • If two answers are similar, except for one or two words, choose one of these.

   • If two quantities or dates are almost the same choose one of those.

   • If two word choices sound similar (basalt, balsa) choose one of those.

   • If dates cover a wide range (1052, 1492, 1865) choose the one in the middle.

2. Use *Steal It*—recognize and use names, dates, and places in other questions as clues to help answer more difficult questions.

3. Read the stem with each option to see which answer best fits or sounds the most familiar.

4. If all of the above strategies have failed, mark the question and leave it for later. (Sometimes the answer will "float" into working memory when ignored, or another question will trigger the answer.)

5. If there is no penalty for guessing and you still cannot answer the question when you return to it, close your eyes and pick an answer. You will be correct about 12 percent of the time.

MICOLUCCI'S TIME MANAGEMENT CHECKLIST

The Time Management Checklist strategy provides students with a process that allows them to record assignments and plan for task completion. *Assignment Tracking* and *Grade Tracking* are necessary companion strategies for the time management strategy to be most successful.

STEPS

1. The student, with the guidance of the teacher, brainstorms a list of critical steps for academic success.

2. The student or teacher types up the list in the form of a checklist and places the checklist in the assignment notebook (or another specific location).

3. The student uses the checklist daily to organize and plan his or her time.

EXAMPLE

Teacher	Subject	Checklist
Jones	Algebra I	☐ Completed all homework on time ☐ Accurately completed assignment book ☐ Practiced at a set time each day ☐ Identified up coming assignments ☐ Planned for completion of assignments ☐ Kept track of grades
Smith	9th English	☐ Completed all homework on time ☐ Accurately completed assignment book ☐ Asked someone to edit essays ☐ Identified up coming assignments ☐ Planned steps for long-term projects ☐ Kept track of grades

Contributed by George Micolucci, May 1999.

WOOMER'S HARD-TO-EASY METHOD OF PRIORITIZING

A prioritizing strategy provides the student with a decision-making routine that identifies the work that needs to be done first. This method is designed for students who routinely complete easy tasks first and avoid engaging in the more difficult tasks. The students need to have developed skill in recording a correct task list (see *Assignment Tracking*) before they can effectively set priorities.

STEPS

1. Create a daily list of all the work that you have been assigned.

2. Determine which items on the list are the most difficult. These are the tasks that will take a lot of time or require someone's help or explanation. Mark those with a capital H.

3. Determine which items are easy and can be done independently. These tasks are important but will not take very much time nor require someone's help or explanation. Mark those with a capital E.

4. Go back through your list and schedule time to complete all the H tasks when a helping person will be nearby.

5. As you complete each H task, cross it off your list. Then do one E task and cross it off.

6. At the end of the day, evaluate your performance:

    • Look for any H task you did not complete.

    • Look for assignments that repeatedly show up as H tasks and never get done.

    • Discuss with someone what causes these tasks to be ignored.

    • Identify the characteristics of the task that makes it difficult.

Contributed by Jon Woomer, May 1997.

GRADE TRACKING

The Grade Tracking strategy provides students with a way to record the grades that they earn. This strategy works especially well for students who have difficulty seeing the "big" picture, students who tend to remember only the good news, and students who only increase their effort during the last two weeks of a marking period. The strategy requires students to record grades as they receive them and to use that information to determine which courses need the most attention.

STEPS

1. Given a record sheet, establish a grade goal for each class and record that information.

2. At least once a day, record grades received by class in an assignment notebook or on a grade sheet.

3. Calculate the current grade in each class at regular intervals. Daily calculation may be needed for some students; others may need to calculate their current averages weekly.

4. Use the liaison report or a teacher conference to confirm the accuracy of the student's information at regular intervals.

5. Compare the current grade average to the goals and identify the subjects that are below the goal.

6. Form a Plan of Action for that course.

7. Repeat the process.

EXAMPLE

SUBJECT:			
TERM:	GOAL:		
TEACHER:			
DATE	ASSIGNMENT	GRADE	CURRENT AVERAGE

CONFERENCING

The Conferencing strategy provides the student with a strategy for interacting cooperatively with teachers, parents, and peers. Learning this process enables the student to gain and share information. When this strategy is learned, it can be used to reinforce skills, to gain feedback on progress, to externalize thought processes, and to increase understanding—all essential components of self-efficacy. Conferencing can serve as a catalyst for the creation of new ideas, as well as encouraging reflection and revision. Students need to be proficient in *Accepting Feedback* and the use of positive self-talk such as the *I Can* strategy before Conferencing can be used. Some associated strategies, such as *Responding to Persuasion* or *Following Instructions* may need to precede this strategy.

STEPS

1. Determine the purpose of the conference (discussion, problem solving, training, tell back, feedback, progress report, etc.)

2. Listen carefully—takes notes, nod your head, or say "mm-hmm" so that the others in the conference know that you are listening.

3. Ask questions about anything that you do not understand. Do not argue or insist on your own way.

4. Using "I" messages that are empty of personal criticism, offer your ideas, opinions, or suggestions. Do not argue or insist on your own way.

5. Decide which ideas, information, suggestions you intend to use and let the other person know.

6. Keep a record of the conference.

FOLLOWING DIRECTIONS

The Following Directions strategy teaches students to comply with the teacher's classroom instructions or the requests of another person.

STEPS

1. Listen carefully without interrupting while the directions are being given. Take notes if necessary, make eye contact or say "mm-hmm" so that the other person knows that you are listening.

2. Ask questions about anything that you don't understand so that the instructions are specific and clear.

3. Repeat the instructions to yourself.

4. Do what you have been instructed to do.

DISTRIBUTED STUDY PROCESS

Distributed Study (as opposed to massed study) provides the student with a review routine that emphasizes the importance of learning material periodically throughout a unit of study. The reviews or "study" sessions are spread into daily reviews, weekly reviews, and major reviews. The major reviews occur a day or two before a major test and five days before an exam. However, the bulk of the memorization is done during the daily and weekly reviews, well before the test or exam.

STEPS

1. Daily reviews: (5 to 10 minutes)
   - Concentrate on memorizing material you have just learned.
   - Read or recite the material just presented in class.
   - Make flash cards, complete Cornell notes, etc., on that information.
   - Do a quick check on your memory of the information learned previously.

2. Weekly reviews: (30 to 45 minutes)
   - Check your memory for all information presented to date.
   - Separate information you know from the information still not in memory.
   - Use a memory strategy for the information still not in long-term memory.
   - Add any missing information to new flash cards, Cornell notes, etc.
   - Create a memory for each item.
   - Check your memory again.
   - Separate the facts that are in memory from those that are not yet stored.

3. Major reviews: (45 to 60 minutes, 2 days in a row before tests, 5 days in a row before exams)
   - Begin the review with the information that has been the most difficult for you to retain.
   - Check your memory for all facts—even those you are sure you have in long-term memory.
   - Separate information that does not leap to mind immediately.
   - Study for 20 minutes then take a short 5-minute break.
   - Create memories for the difficult information again.
   - Repeat this process until the hour is up or the information is easily retrieved.

COVER AND RECITE
(REHEARSAL AND RETRIEVAL PRACTICE)

The Cover and Recite strategy provides students who prefer to study alone with a method of checking their test readiness and to practice retrieving information from their memory. This method of covering, reciting, and checking works well as long as students do not fool themselves into believing information is in long-term memory when it is not. If a student does not know the answer when it is covered, but the response is familiar when uncovered, the information is not yet in long-term memory and needs to be rehearsed. It should be noted that this method of studying could be used for both rehearsal and retrieval, but must be done *ad nauseam*. This strategy differs from "going over" information, which is the most common method of studying as reported by students. If "going over" information was an excellent rehearsal strategy, grades on tests would be much better then they are.

STEPS

1. After deciding on a system of marking correct and incorrect answers, cover the answer and read the question you have prepared.

2. Answer the question and then reveal the correct response. Compare your response with the correct answer and note it in some way. (List right and wrong answers, stars and checks, two separate piles, etc.)

3. Choose a rehearsal strategy that matches your learning style, and use it to learn the information that you got wrong or did not know.

4. Repeat the process.

ORAL RETRIEVAL

Oral Retrieval is a process for checking test readiness using an auditory strategy. Students employ this method when they ask someone to quiz them. The vocalization of the information further reinforces memory. The purpose of Oral Retrieval is to decide readiness for testing or the need for further preparation. Care must be taken that the "testing pairs" switch roles. Testing pairs are most successful when they share common academic, not social, goals. Rehearsal and retrieval strategies should not be used simultaneously. Information that is not in long-term memory should be noted in some fashion, and a rehearsal strategy should be used at a later time.

STEPS

1. After deciding on a system of making correct and incorrect answers, give your list, graphic organizer, flip pack, flash cards on a ring to a study partner.

2. One study partner reads the question (or reveals the question in some way for a visual learner) and the other partner tries answering.

3. Correct, wrong, or unknown responses are noted in some way— lists, stars, checks, two separate piles, etc.

4. If both partners are taking the test, switch roles and repeat the process.

5. Choose a rehearsal strategy that matches your learning style, and use it to learn the items that you got wrong or did not know.

RESPONDING TO PERSUASION

The Responding to Persuasion process instructs the student in a strategy that promotes listening with an open mind and enables the student to separate ideas from personality.

STEPS

1. Listen to the other person's ideas on a topic without interrupting. Make eye contact or say "mm-hmm" so that the other person knows that you are listening.

2. Repeat the other person's ideas in your own words beginning with, "So, what you are telling me is…."

3. Decide what you think about the topic and say your ideas aloud.

4. Compare what the other person said with your ideas.

5. Decide one of the following things and share it with the other person:

    • I agree with your ideas because…

    • I disagree with your ideas because…

    • I would modify your idea this way…

    • I would like more time to think about your ideas I will get back to you on…

KEY WORD PICTURES

This rehearsal strategy uses substitution, imagery, association, and humor to remember information. It is used when large amounts of information need to be retained, or when a concept or fact cannot be easily pictured or associated with prior knowledge. This strategy has the added benefit of being appropriate for any style of learner. Visual learners can make the images bold and colorful, auditory learners can include sounds, and kinesthetic learners can include movement.

STEPS

1. Select a word that has no meaning for you or that you are having trouble retaining.

2. Associate the sound of the word or the look of the word with a vivid, silly, or strange image that is linked to the unknown word.

3. Practice using the image to recall the true meaning of the word or to recognize the true meaning of the word on a test.

EXAMPLES

To remember that John Kay invented the Flying Shuttle, picture a giant white "K" with huge angel wings flying through the blue sky.

To remember that a crab belongs to the crustacean family, picture a crab holding a huge crust of bread in its claw as it walks down the beach.

To remember that "roja" is red in Spanish, picture a huge red rose laughing: Ha, Ha.

GUIDELINES

1. Make the image large and exaggerated.
2. Make the image move, speak, or sing.
3. Make the image bizarre, silly, and unusual.
4. Make the image resonate with sounds similar to the word to be remembered.

SPLASHDOWN

The Splashdown technique is a memorization/rehearsal strategy that students can use during the test itself. As soon as students receive the test, information, such as formulas, associations, and lists, are written directly on the test and used for references during the test. The strategy must be consciously created during the rehearsal stages of the *Objective Test-Taking Cycle* and then used during the test. The students must intend to use this method, have identified what will be important to prepare as a splashdown, and to have practiced writing the information before the test.

STEPS

1. Determine what information will be helpful as a guide during a test (math formulas or steps, memory joggers and associations used, abbreviations, etc.) and write the information on notebook paper, index card, or a sticky note.

2. Practice writing the information quickly from short-term memory. This should take no more than one or two minutes.

3. Take the written splashdown with you to the test. Refer to it until the instructor tells you to put it away.

4. As soon as the test is handed out and before looking at the test questions, jot down as much of the splashdown as you remember.

5. Use the information on your splashdown as a reference as you take the test. Include more information in mini-splashdowns as they occur to you.

GOAL VISUALIZATION

The Goal Visualization strategy provides the students with a process of affirmation when they are working toward the achievement of personal goals. When students have established their own goals, they are more likely to hold themselves responsible for fulfilling those goals, and the goals become self-evaluative motivators. When building self-efficacy, have students periodically visualize themselves achieving those goals, especially when they are working toward difficult goals. The frequency with which Goal Visualization needs to be done varies from student to student.

STEPS

1. Retrieve a copy of the goal.
2. Sit comfortably in a chair with both feet flat on the floor with your hands in you lap.
3. Read the goal, breath deeply three times, and close your eyes.
4. Picture yourself achieving your goals.
5. Describe the positive payoff and the feelings associated with the goal achievement.

RELAX WITH BLACK

The Relax with Black strategy provides the student with a process for reducing stress during a high-stakes activity, such as an exam or test, or during anxiety-producing activities, such as a college or job interview. This strategy should be taught during a period of low stress. The student may need to be cued to use the strategy during several trials before it becomes automatic.

STEPS

1. Close eyes and take a cleansing breath.
2. Hold hands and arms in a relaxed position.
3. Clear the mind of all intruding thoughts by visualizing only a black surface.
4. Every time an interfering visual creeps onto the black surface, erase it.
5. Return to black.
6. Take a cleansing breath and open eyes.

STEAL IT

The Steal It strategy gives the student an increasing sense of control by using the instructions, assignment directions, and previous questions to produce the best possible test answers, compositions, and topic sentences. The process of increasing attention to cues, signals, and the environment heightens the sense of control and self-efficacy.

STEPS

1. Read the question or directions.

2. Use as many of the words and ideas from the directions and questions as possible when composing your topic sentence or your thesis statement.

3. Turn the question into a statement and use that as your first sentence in a paragraph or essay.

4. Use previous test questions or directions to answer other questions.

5. Use grammar cues and clues to choose the best possible answer.

POST-IT PROCESS

The Post-It Process provides students with a strategy for having main ideas, questions, examples, information, and supporting details readily accessible and near the appropriate passages of a school text. It is a concrete way for students to interact with a text without defacing the property. This strategy can be used in conjunction with any of the paraphrasing or comprehension frameworks such as *Math Assault, Muscle Reading, Graphic Organizers,* or memorization strategies such as *Key Word Pictures.*

STEPS

1. Read text silently or subvocally.

2. On a Post-It, paraphrase the main idea, definition, or steps in a process.

    or

    Write a question that needs to be clarified or explained.

3. Place the Post-It near the section of the text or slightly off the page to serve as a place marker.

4. Use the Post-It during class discussion or guided practice or as a reminder to ask for clarification of information.

5. Peel the Post-It off the text and use it in conjunction with the appropriate memorization or comprehension strategy.

ASSIGNMENT TRACKING

The Assignment Tracking strategy provides the student with a way to record the assignments that they have been given. This strategy works especially well for large tasks that seem overwhelming. Students who tend to put off tasks that cannot be done quickly and never experience the satisfaction of completing difficult work will find this helpful. The strategy requires students to break assignments into small manageable pieces, to distinguish between completed work and work that still needs to be done at home, and to set a schedule for completing the unfinished work.

STEPS

1. All daily assignments are recorded in an assignment notebook.

2. Any assignments that are not completed by the end of the school day are highlighted.

3. Any long-term assignments are divided into small subtasks. Then, working back from the due date, students set a schedule for completing the work.

GUIDING QUESTIONS

1. "What should you do the night before (due date) to have the (project) ready?" (This should be cosmetic "polishing"—*no* major work.)

2. "Back up one day. What do you need to have completed this night to have only polishing work tomorrow?" (This needs to be an editing process—correcting errors from some type of editing process or comparing work to a rubric.)

3. "Back up one day. To know what errors need to be corrected tomorrow, what needs to happen on this day?" (This step needs to include someone, other than the student, editing the work and checking the work against the teacher's criteria.)

4. And so on until present day... (Guide student in dividing the work into 30- to 90-minute chunks by asking "How long will that take you to complete?" at each step.)

5. As work progresses, the teacher should inquire about how well the students are keeping to the planned schedule.

6. Teachers should also teach students how to replan—how to change a schedule when tasks take more or less time than expected.

MATERIALS CHECKLIST STRATEGY

The Materials Checklist strategy provides the student with a systematic process of preparing to come to school, go to class, or leave school for home with all the materials necessary to successfully participate in class and to complete assigned work. The checklist should be customized for the individual student so that he or she can arrive at a task with all the necessary materials needed.

STEPS

1. The student, with the guidance of the teacher, brainstorms all the materials needed for a typical day at school.

2. The student or teacher types up the list in the form of a checklist and places the checklist in a location where the student will readily see it.

3. The student compares the checklist against the notebook or book bag before leaving school for home, home for school, or before class and fills in any missing materials.

EXAMPLE

Student: _____

Do I have the following in my book bag?

Two or more pencils	Folders for each subject
Eraser	My homework for each subject
Two or more pens	Spiral notebook for each subject
Notebook paper	Textbooks for each homework assignment
Phone # of my study partner	Assignment notebook

A variation of the Materials Checklist can be used to systematically check work for those students who rush, fail to notice details, or who repeatedly make the same errors.

Math Checklist

1. Did I copy the problem correctly?	5. Did I follow the order of operations?
2. Did I highlight the signs?	6. Did I answer the question?
3. Did I record my *Splashdown*?	7. Is my answer near my estimate?
4. Did I label my answer?	

ATTENTION TAPE PROCESS

The Attention Tape Process provides students with a method of monitoring and charting their attention while performing a task that requires interacting with a text, such as reading for understanding. This process is also useful for students who have Attention Deficit Disorder, when they are doing any task that is not intrinsically motivating and can be used in any academic discipline.

STEPS

1. Make a tape recording that is completely silent except for a sound at odd intervals. The recommended time-interval pattern for a 30-minute tape is 3, 4, 3, 5, 4, 2, 4, 3, and 2 minutes. The sound should be pleasant and not jarring.

2. The students are instructed to begin work as the tape begins.

3. Each time the students hear the sound, they ask, "Am I on task?" and record a yes or no on a simple score sheet.

At the end of the study period (no more than 30 minutes), students total the time they were on task.

During subsequent study times, the students attempt to improve their on-task behavior.

ATTENTION TAPE RECORD

Student _____

Date	Yes	No
3		
4		
3		
5		
4		
2		
4		
3		
2		
Total all yes		

Date	Yes	No
3		
4		
3		
5		
4		
2		
4		
3		
2		
Total all yes		

Date	Yes	No
3		
4		
3		
5		
4		
2		
4		
3		
2		
Total all yes		

Date	Yes	No
3		
4		
3		
5		
4		
2		
4		
3		
2		
Total all yes		

Date	Yes	No
3		
4		
3		
5		
4		
2		
4		
3		
2		
Total all yes		

Date	Yes	No
3		
4		
3		
5		
4		
2		
4		
3		
2		
Total all yes		

APPENDIX II

FORMS

ACCOMMODATIONS

Name _____   Date_____

Disability _____

My Academic Strengths	Successful Strategies

My Learning Needs	Successful Accommodations or Bypass Strategies

Explain how your learning styles and intelligence strength affect your learning:

ACCOMMODATIONS CHECKLIST

(Adapted from Thurlow, M. L., Elliott, J. L., Ysseldyke, J. E. (1998). *Testing Students with Disabilities: Practical Strategies for Complying with District and State Requirements.* Thousand Oaks, CA: Corwin Press.)

Use the following checklist as a starting point to identify appropriate accommodations by answering the following questions about the student.

PRESENTATION

Yes	No	
☐	☐	1. Makes errors when reading silently.
☐	☐	2. Makes reading errors that cause misinterpretations of test questions.
☐	☐	3. Needs clarification of instruction, questions to answer correctly.
☐	☐	4. Distracted or overstimulated by densely typed text.
☐	☐	5. Can read text independently if text is enlarged.
☐	☐	6. Needs questions, directions paraphrased, simplified, or reworded to respond correctly.
☐	☐	7. Needs key words in directions and texts highlighted to identify critical information.
☐	☐	8. Omits or ignores parts of text without visual prompts.
☐	☐	9. Other _____

RESPONSE

Yes	No	
☐	☐	1. Can answer or compose significantly better when using a scribe.
☐	☐	2. Makes errors in the transfer of information from text to worksheet to answer sheet.
☐	☐	3. Does significantly better when allowed to physically cross out and eliminate options.
☐	☐	4. Makes patterns with bubble sheet answers.
☐	☐	5. Has difficulty filling in bubble sheets.
☐	☐	6. Other _____

SETTING

Yes	No	
☐	☐	1. Cannot work independently in a content classroom.
☐	☐	2. Needs assistance to complete written tasks.
☐	☐	3. Distracts others during assessment procedures.
☐	☐	4. Is highly distracted by noise or movement.
☐	☐	5. Can work in content classroom with a noise or movement buffer.
☐	☐	6. Performs best in a small group.
☐	☐	7. Other _____

INSTRUCTIONAL

Yes	No	
☐	☐	1. Has a limited knowledge of organizational and study strategies.
☐	☐	2. Needs guided practice in using self-management strategies.
☐	☐	3. Needs cues and verbal prompts to use strategies.
☐	☐	4. Other _____

SCHEDULING

Yes	No	
☐	☐	1. Has significant difficulty completing tasks in the same length of time as peers.
☐	☐	2. Does significantly better on daily or weekly assessments.
☐	☐	3. Can only work continuously for minutes.
☐	☐	4. Can complete tasks well if provided with periodic breaks.
☐	☐	5. Has periods during the day when medication has dissipated.
☐	☐	6. Other _____

ASSISTIVE DEVICES

Yes   No

☐   ☐   1. Can respond independently only when provided with the following device:

      Yes   No

      ☐   ☐   Calculator

      ☐   ☐   Spell checker

      ☐   ☐   Manipulative

      ☐   ☐   Pencil grip

      ☐   ☐   Page turner

      ☐   ☐   Computer

      ☐   ☐   Adaptive furniture

      ☐   ☐   Text talker converter

      ☐   ☐   Speech synthesizer

      ☐   ☐   Amplification device

      ☐   ☐   Brailler

      ☐   ☐   Tape recorder

      ☐   ☐   Magnification device

      ☐   ☐   Dictionary

      ☐   ☐   Other _____

MOTIVATIONAL

Yes   No

☐   ☐   1. Needs on-task reminders to complete tasks.

☐   ☐   2. Needs verbal prompts to recall information.

☐   ☐   3. Needs encouragement to sustain effort

☐   ☐   4. Needs cues or prompts to begin tasks.

☐   ☐   5. Gets "stuck" and needs prompts to go forward.

☐   ☐   6. Needs prompts to complete tasks that are not perfect.

☐   ☐   7. Needs cues to slow down or go back to complete skipped or missed information.

☐   ☐   8. Needs homework book check for accuracy in order to complete assigned work.

☐   ☐   9. Needs long-term projects periodically checked to complete them on time.

☐   ☐   10. Other _____

ASSIGNMENT NOTEBOOK GRADING SHEET

Student _____

1st Marking Period

Contents	*week 1*	*week 2*	*week 3*	*week 4*	*week 5*	*week 6*	*week 7*	*week 8*
1. Dated at least one month ahead								
2. Assignments recorded								
3. Grades recorded								
4. Long-term projects broken down								
5. Test preparation broken down								
TOTALS								

2nd Marking Period

Contents	*week 1*	*week 2*	*week 3*	*week 4*	*week 5*	*week 6*	*week 7*	*week 8*
1. Dated at least one month ahead								
2. Assignments recorded								
3. Grades recorded								
4. Long-term projects broken down								
5. Test preparation broken down								
TOTALS								

3rd Marking Period

Contents	week 1	week 2	week 3	week 4	week 5	week 6	week 7	week 8
1. Dated at least one month ahead								
2. Assignments recorded								
3. Grades recorded								
4. Long-term projects broken down								
5. Test preparation broken down								
TOTALS								

4th Marking Period

Contents	week 1	week 2	week 3	week 4	week 5	week 6	week 7	week 8
1. Dated at least one month ahead								
2. Assignments recorded								
3. Grades recorded								
4. Long-term projects broken down								
5. Test preparation broken down								
TOTALS								

BRIDGING THE GAP—
FROM OBSTACLES TO SOLUTIONS

Name _____ Date _____

Goal:

Obstacle	Solution

Goal:

Obstacle	Solution

Goal:

Obstacle	Solution

CONFERENCE PLAN/REPORT

Before the meeting:

Agenda	Meeting date/time/place	Participants
	Materials	
Teacher's Positive Theme	Teacher's Strategy/ Suggestion	

During the meeting:

Parent's Needs/Goals	Parent's Problems

Minutes of the Meeting

Decision

After the meeting:

Benefits	What is in the way?

Next Action by Parent	Next Action by Student	Next Action by School

DIFFERENTIATING INSTRUCTION
WITH THE PYRAMID PLANNER

Teacher _____   Unit _____

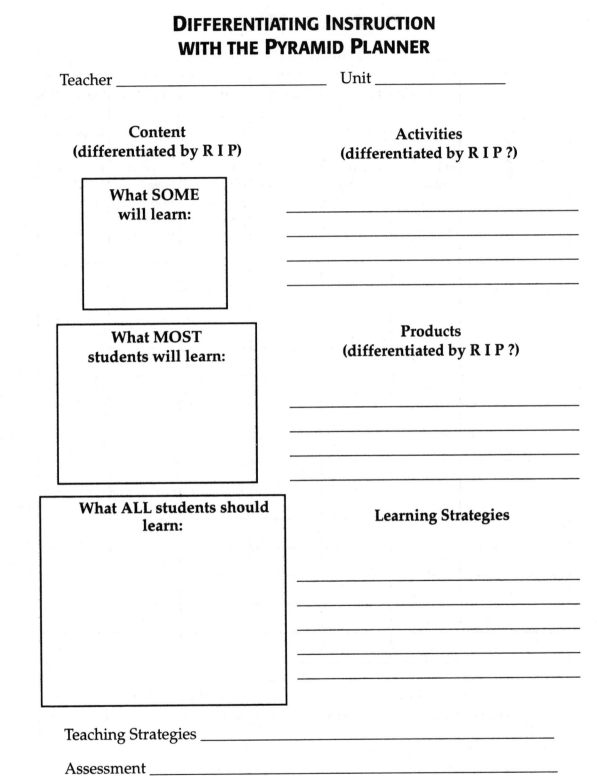

Content
(differentiated by R I P)

What SOME
will learn:

What MOST
students will learn:

What ALL students should
learn:

Activities
(differentiated by R I P ?)

_____

_____

_____

_____

Products
(differentiated by R I P ?)

_____

_____

_____

_____

Learning Strategies

_____

_____

_____

_____

_____

Teaching Strategies _____

Assessment _____

EVIDENCE OF MASTERY

Teacher _____ Date _____ Class ____ Unit _____

Students	Knowledge	Compre-hension	Applica-tion	Analysis	Synthesis	Evaluation
	Identify & recall of infor-mation	Organiza-tion & selection of fact or ideas	Uses facts, rules, principles	Separa-tion of whole into com-ponent parts	Combina-tion of ideas to form a new whole	Judges or decides based on identified criteria

Level of Mastery	Method of Evaluation
√ Has demonstrated proficiency of learner outcomes	P = performance assessment
+ In progress on learner outcomes	A = assignment
− Has not yet demonstrated proficiency of learner outcomes	O = observation
	% = test (percentage correct)

EXPECTATIONS

Name _____ Date _____

People have expectations that influence our behaviors. Often the expectations we have for ourselves come from the expectations that others have for us. These expectations influence our behaviors in both positive and negative ways.

Directions:

1. Identify three people in your life who hold expectations for you. Using magazines or personal drawings, find a picture or symbol of each person. Be sure to include yourself on the list.

2. Affix the pictures to a page in your Thinking Journal, and write an expectations statement that each would have of you.

3. Develop a response statement that each would have if you improved your self-efficacy skills, and write it below each picture.

4. Write a paragraph in your journal describing your feelings about meeting the expectations of the people in your life.

FROM STRENGTHS AND WEAKNESSES TO GOALS

Name _____ Date _____

Strengths—list at least four things you know and do that lead to school success	**Weaknesses**—list at least four things you do or habits you have that get in the way of school success

Goal-Setting Activity

Directions: Set three goals for the marking period. Each goal must be specific, clear, and challenging but attainable through your own efforts. Each goal must be something that is important to you and that you are willing to work toward achieving.

1. _____

2. _____

3. _____

Why are these goals important to you? _____

_____

_____

What will you need to do differently to achieve your goals? _____

_____

_____

GOAL-SETTING PYRAMID

Student _____ Date _____

One long-term
goal—Achievable by
the end of the school term

1. _____

_____

Two mid-term goals—Achievable by
the end of the current semester

1. _____

_____

2. _____

_____

Three short-term goals—Achievable by the
end of the current marking period

1. _____

_____

2. _____

_____

3. _____

_____

1. These goals are important to me because _____

_____

2. My reward for achieving these goals will be _____

_____

3. I will share my goals with _____

_____

4. I will know I have achieved my goals when _____

_____

GOAL VISUALIZATION—
IMAGINE THE POSSIBILITIES

Name _____ Date _____

Directions: Often the language we use guides our behavior and shapes the possibilities we believe we have. In this exercise, you will hunt for any negative words that you are using as road blocks to your academic success and then relax and visualize yourself completing what *you* intend to accomplish.

1. List several academic goals you intended to achieve since school began.

   _____

   _____

   _____

2. Reread your list and highlight words like "hope," "try," "harder," "good," and "study." These words are vague or have very little specific, concrete meaning. They sound good, but do not identify any specific action or intention. Consider how you might sabotage your own intentions. You know yourself better than anyone does. How might you be causing your own failures?

   _____

   _____

   _____

3. Write what you intend to do between now and the end of the semester. Avoid writing in the negative (what you will not do) and avoid using the words from #2. State exactly what you intend to do and how you will know if you have done it. Make your intentions dependent on you alone.

   _____

   _____

   _____

4. Visualize yourself achieving your intentions. Think about one of the specific goals you have written. Sit comfortably in your chair and gently close your eyes. Imagine yourself completing the goal. Write an affirmation statement that says that you completed the goal you just visualized.

   _____

   _____

   _____

INTENTIONS—
WHERE DO WE GO FROM HERE?

Name _____ Date _____

Directions: Personal goal achievement is not easy especially if the goals you have set for yourself involve effort. Planning is required if you are to succeed. This evaluation will help you look at your progress thus far and help you decide if you are taking the steps necessary to achieve challenging goals.

1. Locate the goals you developed for this semester and reread the journal entries you made about your goals.

2. Prepare a journal entry using the following guidelines:

   • Put today's date on the top of the page and restate your short-term objectives.

   • Contrast your intended strategies (action plan) with what you actually did and write about activities or feelings that got in the way. Why did they get in the way? What will you need to do differently?

   • Write about what helped you. How are you feeling about your progress and the opportunities in the rest of the school year?

3. Write four specific actions you intend to take during the next marking period.

   I intend to _____
   _____

   I intend to _____
   _____

   I intend to _____
   _____

   I intend to _____
   _____

4. Give your journal and your intentions to the instructor for a response, and schedule a conference to explain your intentions.

THINKING SKILLS LIKERT SCALE

(Adapted from the Unionville High School Thinking Skills Project.)

Date _____ Grade _____ Subject _____ Teacher _____

Indicator*	Always (5)	Usually (4)	Some-times (3)	Occa-sionally (2)	Not Yet (1)	Not Ap-plicable (0)	Comments, Observations, Evidence
Perserverance	5 . . . . . . 4 . . . . . 3 . . . . . . 2 . . . . . . .1 0						
Decreased impulsivity	5 . . . . . . 4 . . . . . 3 . . . . . . 2 . . . . . . .1 0						
Flexibility	5 . . . . . . 4 . . . . . 3 . . . . . . 2 . . . . . . .1 0						
Metacognition	5 . . . . . . 4 . . . . . 3 . . . . . . 2 . . . . . . .1 0						
Careful review	5 . . . . . . 4 . . . . . 3 . . . . . . 2 . . . . . . .1 0						
Problem posing	5 . . . . . . 4 . . . . . 3 . . . . . . 2 . . . . . . .1 0						
Past knowledge	5 . . . . . . 4 . . . . . 3 . . . . . . 2 . . . . . . .1 0						
Enjoyment of problem solving	5 . . . . . . 4 . . . . . 3 . . . . . . 2 . . . . . . .1 0						
Precise language	5 . . . . . . 4 . . . . . 3 . . . . . . 2 . . . . . . .1 0						

* See page 157 for definition, observable behaviors, and prompts for these indicators.

CHARACTERISTIC	DESCRIPTION	BEHAVIOR	CUES/PROMPTS
Perseverance	Working until solution is reached	Tries again, debates strategy, changes strategies	Look at this again. What else might you try?
Decreased impulsivity	Pausing to reflect or clarify, requesting more information	Asks for facts, pauses before answering	Speed doesn't count. Gather your thoughts. Take your time.
Flexibility	Considering the other points of view, trying new approaches	Paraphrases others, accepts suggestions or directions, evaluates responses	Can anyone think of another way to... Let's try looking at this another way.
Metacognition	Analyzing, describing one's own thought processes	Retraces steps, describes strategies and processes used	Go through the steps aloud. How did you do that?
Careful review	Proofing work, comparing work to criteria or exemplar	Reflects on accuracy of work, checks to ensure accuracy	Did you compare your work to the rubric? Have you used a peer editor?
Problem posing	Asking questions and finding problems to solve	Wonders. Asks for proof or evidence	How do you know? What would happen if...?
Past knowledge	Using prior knowledge or past learning	Makes connection to past experience, content or ideas	Does this remind you of anything else? Where else might this be useful?
Enjoyment of problem solving	Solving problems with increasing joy and independence	Positive comments. On task for extended period of time.	You're doing great. Keep working. I'm pleased to see you're hanging in there.
Precise language	Using appropriate descriptive words and labels	Uses analogies, complete sentences. Concise.	Stop and think first. What is the scientific word for that?

LONG-TERM PROJECT GOAL SETTING

Name _____ Date _____

Directions: Follow the six steps below to identify your science fair goals and to visualize your self completing what you intend to accomplish.

1. In your _____ journal, write your goal for the _____ project.

   - Be positive about what you intend to do and be willing to take a risk.

   - Challenge yourself but be realistic—give yourself the opportunity to succeed.

   - Break your largest goal into a series of smaller goals—What is your goal for this week? And for next week?

2. Break your goal into a series of intention—What you intend to do between now and the due date to achieve your goal.

   - Avoid writing in the negative—don't tell what you will not do.

   - Leave out words like "hope," "try," "harder," or "good."

   - Be specific about what you intend to do—What will it look like?

3. Set deadlines for each of your intentions and record each step in your assignment notebook.

4. Consider how you might sabotage your own intentions.

   - Have you made your goals dependent on you alone?

   - How might you cause your own failure?

   - What are the chances of you achieving your goals?

5. Relax, close your eyes, and picture yourself completing what you intended to accomplish.

   - Notice how you feel.

6. Write a goal affirmation sentence in your journal.

MUSCLE-READING BOOKMARK

MUSCLE-READING BOOKMARK

Phase I—POP

Preview (*look*)—pictures, chapter review, vocabulary list

Outline (*choose one*)—highlight, Post-It's, Cornell notes, list, flash cards

Pose Questions (*think*)— headings, bold words, section headings, homework

Phase II—RAP

Read (*slowly*)—visualize, recite, slow down, request help

Accent (*write as you go*)

Puzzle (*check and fill in*)— answer the questions

Phase III—ROAR

Recall (*explain all you know*)

Review (*memorize*)—key word pictures, do and redo, walk about, cover and recite

Review (*memory check*)

Repeat (*do Phase III again*)

MUSCLE-READING BOOKMARK

Phase I—POP

Preview (*look*)—pictures, chapter review, vocabulary list

Outline (*choose one*)—highlight, Post-It's, Cornell notes, list, flash cards

Pose Questions (*think*)— headings, bold words, section headings, homework

Phase II—RAP

Read (*slowly*)—visualize, recite, slow down, request help

Accent (*write as you go*)

Puzzle (*check and fill in*)— answer the questions

Phase III—ROAR

Recall (*explain all you know*)

Review (*memorize*)—key word pictures, do and redo, walk about, cover and recite

Review (*memory check*)

Repeat (*do Phase III again*)

OBJECTIVE TEST-TAKING CYCLE

Steps	*Possible Strategies*			*Personal Plan*
1. Set Goal: target a grade establish a time frame commit to strategies	Conferencing	Journalizing	Pyramid	
2. Identify the key information	Graphic Organizer Clustering Math Attack Color Coding	Cued Notes Highlighting Flash cards Skimming	3-Fold Page Cornell Notes Post-It's Muscle Reading	
3. Memorize the information	Walk About Do & Redo Acronyms Oral Rehearsal	Study Partner Peer Teacher Splashdown 3-Fold Page	Overlearning Write/Read Key Word Pictures	
4. Check memory	Practice Test Oral Retrieval Walk About	Study Partner 3-Fold Page Flash cards	Cover & Recite Splashdown Computer drill	
5. Adjust target grade	Reward Yourself	Goal Setting	Accepting Feedback	
6. Repeat Steps 3 to 5	I will repeat: 1 2 3 4 5 times			
7. Take test	Visualizations Eliminate Options Peek-a-boo Using Margins	Splashdown Steal It Triage Easy to Hard	Oral Retrieval Cued Notes SCORER Fore/Back	
8. Critique test performance	Reward Yourself Requesting Help	Conclusions Consequences	Skill Evaluation	
9. Adjust Strategies	Responding to Persuasion Decision Making		Responding to Help Requesting Help	
Repeat the cycle				

OBJECTIVE TEST-TAKING PLANNER

Name _____ Date _____

Step	*Strategies*
1. Set goal	1. What grade are you willing to work for?
2. Identify key information	2. How will you separate out the facts that will be on the test?
3. Memorize information	3. How will you get the information into long-term memory?
4. Check memory	4. How will you find out the facts are really in your memory and you can get them out of memory?
5. Adjust target grade	5. How will you know if you are as prepared as you wish to be?
6. Repeat Steps 3 to 5	6. How many times will you repeat Steps 3, 4, and 5 before the test?
7. Take test	7. What strategies will you use during the test?
8. Critique performance	8. How will you figure out what went right and what went wrong?
9. Adjust strategies	9. How will you prepare for the next test?

Repeat the Cycle

QUESTIONS TO ASK

Questions to ask students before the task

1. What do you think this lesson is about?
2. What are you to do in the lesson? Can you show me? Can you tell me?
3. Do you think you can do the task? If not, why not?
4. What do you already know about the topic?

Questions to ask student during the task

1. Tell me or show me what you are doing.
2. If you are unsure of what to do, how do you get help?
3. Talk to me about what you are learning.
4. What do you do when you do not understand something?
5. Is what you are doing easy or hard? Why?

Questions to ask students after the task

1. What did you learn from the lesson? about this topic?
2. Did you correctly predict what the lesson would be about?
3. What helped you to understand the lesson or topic?
4. How will you remember what you have learned?
5. How will you use what you have learned?

Adapted from Gickling, E. (1994). *Preparation for Adult Life*,
Secondary Instructional Support Assessment Workshop.
Chester County Intermediate Unit, Exton, PA, Nov. 1997.

REFLECTION—AM I WHERE I WANT TO BE?

Directions: Read your marking period goals and the strategies you chose to meet those goals. Then use the following questions to guide your preparation for a journal entry.

1. Did you achieve the short-term goals you established for this marking period?

2. What was harder than you expected?

3. What was difficult for you? What excuses did you use to avoid working toward your goals?

4. What did you find most encouraging or helpful?

5. Are you using your strategies regularly? Are they making a difference in your school success?

6. Do you still need to strengthen any strategy categories?

7. Are you as successful as you want to be?

Prepare a journal entry for each of the following questions:

PROGRESS: Have you reached your goals? Why or why not?

FACILITATOR: What is in the way or has slowed you down when you tried to reach your goal?

GROWTH: What did you learn during the marking period that you can use during the next marking period? What skills have you improved since the beginning of this year?

INTENTIONS: What will you do differently from now until the end of this school year so that you can reach the goals that you have set for yourself?

CHANGES: Do you need to change your goals or pick new strategies? Why or why not?

Give your journal to the instructor for a response.

SCORED DISCUSSIONS TALLY SHEET

Student ➜										
Offers position on topic (1)										
Makes a relevant comment (1)										
Uses evidence to support position (3)										
Points out contradictions (2)										
Recognizes irrelevant comments (2)										
Develops analogy (3)										
Asks a clarifying question (1)										
Uses active listening (3)										
Does not pay attention (–1)										
Distracting noises (–2)										
Distracting movements (–1)										
Interrupting (–2)										
Inappropriate humor (–2)										
Monopolizing (–3)										
Personal attacks (–3)										
Irrelevant comments (–1)										
Totals										

SEMESTER EVALUATION

Name _____ Date _____

Directions: Rate each academic area and explain any that are lower than they should be. Give your evaluation to the instructor for feedback and suggestions.

Academic Areas to Consider	Rating	Explanation	Teacher Suggestions
Report Card Grades			
Meeting Deadlines—homework, projects, test preparation			
On Time—to school, to class			
Self-assigned Homework—editing writing, test preparation, perfecting projects, practicing math			
Self-efficacy—knowing and using accommodations, learning style, strategies, accepting feedback, prioritizing			
Goal Attainment—daily, short-term, mid-term, long-term			
Time on Academic Tasks—in school, after school			
Keeping Track—homework, projects, test preparation, materials, grades			

Mastered: I do this automatically. This is part of my school behavior. No one has to remind me.

Good: I know how to do this, but I sometimes have to be reminded. Even though I know this will help me be more successful, I don't do this automatically.

Needs Work: I know I should do this, but I often need to be reminded. I only do this when an adult suggests this or reminds me it needs to be done.

Not Yet: I only do this when I am forced to or when I am being observed.

SETTING AND REFLECTING ON GOALS

1. Self-questioning by _____ Date _____
   - What are some good things that might happen to me if I improve my school performance?
   - What are some bad things that might happen to me if I improve my school performance?
   - What could keep me from improving my school performance?
   - Who can help me improve my school performance?

2. Goal Setting—Each goal must be specific, clear, and challenging but attainable through your own efforts. Each goal much be something that is important to you and that you are willing to work toward achieving.
   - As a short-term goal, I will _____

   _____

   _____
   - As a mid-term goal, I will _____

   _____

   _____
   - As a long-term goal, I will _____

   _____

   _____

3. Affirmation
   - Share your goals with someone you identified as helping you to improve.
   - Explain how you will achieve your goals and what the reward will be.
   - Arrange to meet regularly with the person to discuss your progress.

4. Reflection (think about these things after the meeting with your support person)
   - Were you satisfied with your progress?
   - Were your goals clear and sharp in your mind?
   - Did the support person you used keep you focused and honest?

SKILLS EVALUATION

(The following material continues on the next page.)

Student √ the box that is true of you			Name _____ Date _____	Teacher √ the box that is true of this student		
Mastered	Needs Work	Not Yet		Mastered	Needs Work	Not Yet
			Openness to Instruction			
			Uses suggestions given by teachers			
			Accepts skill instruction from teachers			
			Follows directions given by teacher			
			Quiets self, allows teacher to quiet			
			Asks for instruction and feedback to improve			
			Keeping Track			
			Homework (dates due, location)			
			Projects (dates, steps, rubric)			
			Test preparation (when, how often)			
			Materials (homework, textbooks, pens)			
			Strategy Repertoire			
			Has a variety of ways to study and learn			
			Can explain how to study and work			
			Chooses strategies that match learning style			
			Knows if a strategy is working well			

			Self-Efficacy/Determination/Advocacy			
			Asks for accommodations			
			Knows learning style			
			Knows personal strengths, weaknesses			
			Does the most important work first			
			Sets goals			
			Achieves goals			
			Self-Assigned Work			
			Test preparation			
			Projects			
			Writing, editing, rewriting			
			Organizing notebooks, locker, desk			
			Drill and practice			
			Time Management			
			Uses school time for completing work			
			Has a study routine for after school			
			Arrives on time to school			
			Arrives on time to class			
			Plans time for projects' deadlines			
			Plans time for test preparation			

SKILL EVALUATION CHECKLIST

Requests instruction for difficult work	Uses suggestions given by teacher	Quiets self or allows the teacher to quiet	Accepts feedback from teachers, peers	Has a variety of strategies to choose from	Chooses strategies that match problem	Learns new strategies	Works toward achieving goal	Date _____ Teacher _____
								Students

M = Mastered	Student does this automatically. This is part of the student's school habits. No one has to remind the student to do this.
G = Good	Student can do this but sometimes needs to be reminded. Not an automatic part of this student's behavior.
W = Needs Work	Student knows how to do this but almost always needs someone to remind him or her.
Y = Not Yet	Student cannot do this or refuses to do this.

SMOKE AND MIRRORS

Directions: The process of writing down goals and making them public through an affirmation process dissipates the "smoke" and provides a "mirror" through which you can reflect on your progress.

1. Self-questioning by _____ Date _____
   - What are some good things that might happen to me if I improve my school performance?
   - What are some bad things that might happen to me if I improve my school performance?
   - What could keep me from improving my school performance?
   - Who can help me improve my school performance?

   _____

   _____

   _____

2. Goal Setting—Each goal must be specific, clear, and challenging but attainable through your own efforts. Each goal must be something that is important to you and that you are willing to work toward achieving.
   - As a short-term goal, I will _____
   - As a mid-term goal, I will _____
   - As a long-term goal, I will _____

3. Affirmation
   - Share your goals with someone you identified as helping you to improve.
   - Explain how you will achieve your goals and what the reward will be.
   - Arrange to meet regularly with the person to discuss your progress.
   - My meeting time with my support person will be _____

4. Reflection (think about these things after the meeting with your support person)
   - Were you satisfied with your progress?
   - Were your goals clear and sharp in your mind?
   - Did the support person you used keep you focused and honest?

   _____

   _____

STRATEGIES I NEED!

Student _____ Date _____

Directions: Pick your three most successful strategies, tell why you use it, and then think of a new use for the strategy.

Strategy #1 _____	**I will use this for**
I need this because	

Strategy #2 _____	**I will use this for**
I need this because	

Strategy #3 _____	**I will use this for**
I need this because	

STRATEGIES THAT WORK!

Student _____ Date _____

Directions: Pick your three most successful strategies, tell why you use it, and then think of a new use for the strategy.

Strategy #1 _____ **I used this for:**	**Other uses:**

Strategy #2 _____ **I used this for:**	**Other uses:**

Strategy #3 _____ **I used this for:**	**Other uses:**

STRATEGIES CRITICAL FOR SUCCESS

Name _____	Date _____	
Directions: Highlight the strategies that you are currently using.		**Directions:** Describe how the strategy is contributing to your academic success.
Self-efficacy and Advocacy	Goal setting/achievement Goal Visualization I Can Accepting Feedback Requesting Help Management Checklists Test Critique	
Memorizing	Key Word Pictures Highlighting Oral Rehearsal Oral/Visual Retrieval Study Partner Cover and Recite 3-Fold Page Do & Redo	
Test Taking	Steal It Splashdown Eliminating Options Math Checklist	
Concentrating	Bracketing/Pocketing Chairs in Place Relax with Black Hard-to-Easy Easy First Distributive Study	
Composing	Graphic Organizers Steal It Oral Rehearsal Stop & Think Editing Partner Semantic Mapping	
Understanding	Post-It Process Stop & Think Cornell Note Taking Math Assault Muscle Reading	
Organizing	Assignment Tracking Grade Tracking Hard-to-Easy Prioritizing Materials Checklist Highlighting	

STUDENT SELF-CRITIQUE

Name _____ Date _____

Directions: Complete the critique below and attach to your completed project.

1. I was on the right track with my strategies for planning and completing my project, but what I didn't know was _____

    _____

2. I wish I had known more about _____

    _____

    _____

3. Three things I want you to notice about my project are:

    *   _____

    *   _____

    *   _____

STUDY PLANNER

(The following material continues on the next page.)

Name _____ Date _____ Period _____ Teacher _____

THE HABITS

1. I **organize** myself during the first 5 minutes by making a 40-minute lesson plan that clearly identifies my goals, subjects, assignments, and strategies. I ask someone for assistance if I am unsure of what I need to accomplish.

2. I take responsibility for my **materials** by having all the supplies I need to complete the work I plan.

3. I show **commitment** by working the entire period, asking someone for assistance when I need information or instruction to complete my planned work.

4. I actively participate in my own education by **completing** the work I planned so that I can achieve the goals I have established.

5. I work **independently** but follow the teacher's suggested strategies, frameworks, and processes to improve my self-efficacy habits.

6. I quiet myself and put myself back **on task** or I allow others to put me back on task when I am unable to do so.

7. I **communicate** in an appropriate, confident, polite, clear manner.

THE PLAN

Goal:

_____

Subject: Subject:

_____   _____

Assignment: Assignment:

_____   _____

Strategy: Strategy:

_____   _____

THE SCORE

4 = Mastered   I do this automatically. This is part of my school behavior. No one has to remind me.

3 = Good	I know how to do this, but I sometimes have to be reminded. Even though I know this will help me be more successful, I don't do this automatically.
2 = Needs Work	I know I should do this, but I often need to be reminded. I only do this when an adult suggests this or reminds me it needs to be done.
1 = Not Yet	I only do this when I am forced to or when I am being observed.
0 = Not Ever	I refuse to do this or I do not think this is necessary for me.

	Student	*Teacher*	*Comments:*
1. Organize	_____	_____	_____
2. Materials	_____	_____	_____
3. Commitment	_____	_____	_____
4. Completing	_____	_____	_____
5. Independently	_____	_____	_____
6. On Task	_____	_____	_____
7. Communicate	_____	_____	_____
Total:	_____ +	_____	÷56 = _____%

TEST-TAKING CRITIQUE

Directions: Use this checklist to help identify the obstacles to achieving the grade you want on a test. Draw some conclusions from the analysis and then brainstorm some possible solutions.

Name _____ Subject _____

Test Date _____ Critique Date _____

Predicted Grade _____ Actual Grade _____ Next Target Grade _____

(✖) *Analysis*	(✍) *Conclusions/Possible Solutions*
____ I should have started to prepare sooner than I did.	_____
____ I did not schedule enough time for preparation.	_____
____ I did the teacher-assigned homework and though my preparation was adequate.	_____
____ I should have prepared a splashdown.	_____
____ I should have picked a different strategy for preparation.	_____
____ I prepared for recognition when I needed recall.	_____
____ I was overconfident.	_____
____ I studied the wrong information.	_____
____ I had trouble understanding the questions or instructions.	_____
____ I had trouble with the format of the test.	_____
____ I misinterpreted what some of the questions were asking.	_____
____ I made careless mistakes.	_____
____ I ran out of time.	_____
____ I guessed too much.	_____
____ I choked or "blanked out" during the test.	_____
____ I was unfamiliar with parts of the test.	_____
____ I remember seeing the materials but could not "pull" the information from my memory.	_____
____ Other _____	_____

THINKING JOURNAL PROMPTS

The _____ goal I was most focused on this week was…
        (subject)

It was hard for me to stay focused on my goals because…

As I worked toward achieving my goals, I was surprised to learn…

The strategy that brought me closer to my goals was…

It was more difficult than I thought it would be to…

After I set my goals, it was hard for me to…

My goal for next week is…

As I worked toward my goals, the most encouraging thing for me was…

I discovered the excuse I use to avoid working toward my goal is…

Before I set up my plan, I wish I had been told more about…

My goal for next week is to plan…

I organized all of my materials for class by…

This week was special for me because I am getting better at planning for…

I had some trouble planning for _____, but I solved it by…

I was surprised to learn that planning helped me to…

It was hard for me to learn…

Three strategies that I used today are…

This week I wished I had a better strategy for…

THE WEEK IN REVIEW

Date _____

This week I feel good about _____

_____

because _____ .

_____

This week was easy for me because _____

_____ .

I really had to put effort into _____

_____ .

I had fun when _____

_____ .

My goal next week is to _____

_____

_____

_____ .

Signed,

_____

THE YEAR IN REVIEW

Date _____

This year I feel good about _____

_____

_____ because _____

_____.

This year, I learned _____

_____

_____ and next year I intend to _____

_____.

This year, the strategies that I used most successfully were _____

_____

_____

_____.

The amount of academic support I will need next year is _____

_____

_____ because _____

_____.

Signed,

_____